◆ ANCIENT WORLD LEADERS ◆

ALEXANDER THE GREAT

ATTILA THE HUN

JULIUS CAESAR

CHARLEMAGNE

GENGHIS KHAN

SALADIN

ANCIENT WORLD LEADERS

JULIUS CAESAR

Samuel Willard Crompton

CHELSEA HOUSE
PUBLISHERS
A Haights Cross Communications Company

Philadelphia

Frontispiece: Roman leader Julius Caesar, the dictator who oversaw the end of the Roman republic, is one of the most legendary figures of the ancient world. Few before or since have matched his reputation both in politics or on the battlefield.

CHELSEA HOUSE PUBLISHERS

VP, New Product Development Sally Cheney
Director of Production Kim Shinners
Creative Manager Takeshi Takahashi
Manufacturing Manager Diann Grasse

Staff for JULIUS CAESAR

Associate Editor Benjamin Xavier Kim
Production Editor Jaimie Winkler
Picture Researcher Pat Holl
Series Designer Takeshi Takahashi
Cover Designer Takeshi Takahashi
Layout 21st Century Publishing and Communications, Inc.

A Haights Cross Communications ✦ Company

http://www.chelseahouse.com

First Printing

1 3 5 7 9 8 6 4 2

Library of Congress Cataloging-in-Publication Data

Crompton, Samuel Willard.
    Julius Caesar / by Samuel Willard Crompton.
        p. cm. — (Ancient world leaders)
Includes index.
Summary: A biography of the Roman general and statesman whose brilliant military leadership helped make Rome the center of a vast empire.
    ISBN 0-7910-7220-7
    1. Caesar, Julius—Juvenile literature. 2. Heads of state—Rome—Biography—Juvenile literature. 3. Generals—Rome—Biography—Juvenile literature. 4. Rome—History—Republic, 265-30 B.C.—Juvenile literature. [1. Caesar, Julius. 2. Heads of state. 3. Generals. 4. Rome—History—Republic, 265-30 B.C.] I. Title. II. Series.
DG261 .C84 2002
937'.05'092—dc21

2002015928

TABLE OF CONTENTS

ON LEADERSHIP

Arthur M. Schlesinger, jr.

L eadership, it may be said, is really what makes the world go round. Love no doubt smoothes the passage; but love is a private transaction between consenting adults. Leadership is a public transaction with history. The idea of leadership affirms the capacity of individuals to move, inspire, and mobilize masses of people so that they act together in pursuit of an end. Sometimes leadership serves good purposes, sometimes bad; but whether the end is benign or evil, great leaders are those men and women who leave their personal stamp on history.

Now, the very concept of leadership implies the proposition that individuals can make a difference. This proposition has never been universally accepted. From classical times to the present day, eminent thinkers have regarded individuals as no more than the agents and pawns of larger forces, whether the gods and goddesses of the ancient world or, in the modern era, race, class, nation, the dialectic, the will of the people, the spirit of the times, history itself. Against such forces, the individual dwindles into insignificance.

So contends the thesis of historical determinism. Tolstoy's great novel *War and Peace* offers a famous statement of the case. Why, Tolstoy asked, did millions of men in the Napoleonic Wars, denying their human feelings and their common sense, move back and forth across Europe slaughtering their fellows? "The war," Tolstoy answered, "was bound to happen simply because it was bound to happen." All prior history determined it. As for leaders, they, Tolstoy said, "are but the labels that serve to give a name to an end and, like labels, they have the least possible connection with the event." The greater the leader, "the more conspicuous the inevitability and the predestination of every act he commits." The leader, said Tolstoy, is "the slave of history."

Determinism takes many forms. Marxism is the determinism of class. Nazism the determinism of race. But the idea of men and women as the slaves of history runs athwart the deepest human instincts. Rigid determinism abolishes the idea of human freedom—the assumption of free choice that underlies every move we make, every word we speak, every thought we think. It abolishes the idea of human responsibility, since it is manifestly unfair to reward or punish people for actions that are by definition beyond their control. No one can live consistently by any deterministic creed. The Marxist states prove this themselves by their extreme susceptibility to the cult of leadership.

More than that, history refutes the idea that individuals make no difference. In December 1931 a British politician crossing Fifth Avenue in New York City between 76th and 77th Streets around 10:30 P.M. looked in the wrong direction and was knocked down by an automobile—a moment, he later recalled, of a man aghast, a world aglare: "I do not understand why I was not broken like an eggshell or squashed like a gooseberry." Fourteen months later an American politician, sitting in an open car in Miami, Florida, was fired on by an assassin; the man beside him was hit. Those who believe that individuals make no difference to history might well ponder whether the next two decades would have been the same had Mario Constasino's car killed Winston Churchill in 1931 and Giuseppe Zangara's bullet killed Franklin Roosevelt in 1933. Suppose, in addition, that Lenin had died of typhus in Siberia in 1895 and that Hitler had been killed on the western front in 1916. What would the 20th century have looked like now?

For better or for worse, individuals do make a difference. "The notion that a people can run itself and its affairs anonymously," wrote the philosopher William James, "is now well known to be the silliest of absurdities. Mankind does nothing save through initiatives on the part of inventors, great or small, and imitation by the rest of us—these are the sole factors in human progress. Individuals of genius show the way, and set the patterns, which common people then adopt and follow."

Leadership, James suggests, means leadership in thought as well as in action. In the long run, leaders in thought may well make the greater difference to the world. "The ideas of economists and political philosophers, both when they are right and when they are wrong," wrote John Maynard Keynes, "are more powerful than is commonly understood. Indeed the world is ruled by little else. Practical men, who believe themselves to be quite exempt from any intellectual influences, are usually the slaves of some defunct economist. . . . The power of vested interests is vastly exaggerated compared with the gradual encroachment of ideas."

But, as Woodrow Wilson once said, "Those only are leaders of men, in the general eye, who lead in action. . . . It is at their hands that new thought gets its translation into the crude language of deeds." Leaders in thought often invent in solitude and obscurity, leaving to later generations the tasks of imitation. Leaders in action—the leaders portrayed in this series—have to be effective in their own time.

And they cannot be effective by themselves. They must act in response to the rhythms of their age. Their genius must be adapted, in a phrase from William James, "to the receptivities of the moment." Leaders are useless without followers. "There goes the mob," said the French politician, hearing a clamor in the streets. "I am their leader. I must follow them." Great leaders turn the inchoate emotions of the mob to purposes of their own. They seize on the opportunities of their time, the hopes, fears, frustrations, crises, potentialities. They succeed when events have prepared the way for them, when the community is awaiting to be aroused, when they can provide the clarifying and organizing ideas. Leadership completes the circuit between the individual and the mass and thereby alters history.

It may alter history for better or for worse. Leaders have been responsible for the most extravagant follies and most monstrous crimes that have beset suffering humanity. They have also been vital in such gains as humanity has made in individual freedom, religious and racial tolerance, social justice, and respect for human rights.

There is no sure way to tell in advance who is going to lead for good and who for evil. But a glance at the gallery of men and women in ANCIENT WORLD LEADERS suggests some useful tests.

One test is this: Do leaders lead by force or by persuasion? By command or by consent? Through most of history leadership was exercised by the divine right of authority. The duty of followers was to defer and to obey. "Theirs not to reason why/Theirs but to do and die." On occasion, as with the so-called enlightened despots of the 18th century in Europe, absolutist leadership was animated by humane purposes. More often, absolutism nourished the passion for domination, land, gold, and conquest and resulted in tyranny.

The great revolution of modern times has been the revolution of equality. "Perhaps no form of government," wrote the British historian James Bryce in his study of the United States, *The American Commonwealth*, "needs great leaders so much as democracy." The idea that all people should be equal in their legal condition has undermined the old structure of authority, hierarchy, and deference. The revolution of equality has had two contrary effects on the nature of leadership. For equality, as Alexis de Tocqueville pointed out in his great study *Democracy in America,* might mean equality in servitude as well as equality in freedom.

"I know of only two methods of establishing equality in the political world," Tocqueville wrote. "Rights must be given to every citizen, or none at all to anyone . . . save one, who is the master of all." There was no middle ground "between the sovereignty of all and the absolute power of one man." In his astonishing prediction of 20th-century totalitarian dictatorship, Tocqueville explained how the revolution of equality could lead to the *Führerprinzip* and more terrible absolutism than the world had ever known.

But when rights are given to every citizen and the sovereignty of all is established, the problem of leadership takes a new form, becomes more exacting than ever before. It is easy to issue commands and enforce them by the rope and the stake, the concentration camp and the *gulag.* It is much harder to use argument and achievement to overcome opposition and win consent. The Founding Fathers of the United States understood the difficulty. They believed that history had given them the opportunity to decide, as Alexander Hamilton wrote in the first Federalist Paper, whether men are indeed capable of basing government on "reflection and choice, or whether they are forever destined to depend . . . on accident and force."

Government by reflection and choice called for a new style of leadership and a new quality of followership. It required leaders to be responsive to popular concerns, and it required followers to be active and informed participants in the process. Democracy does not eliminate emotion from politics; sometimes it fosters demagoguery; but it is confident that, as the greatest of democratic leaders put it, you cannot fool all of the people all of the time. It measures leadership by results and retires those who overreach or falter or fail.

It is true that in the long run despots are measured by results too. But they can postpone the day of judgment, sometimes indefinitely, and in the meantime they can do infinite harm. It is also true that democracy is no guarantee of virtue and intelligence in government, for the voice of the people is not necessarily the voice of God. But democracy, by assuring the right of opposition, offers built-in resistance to the evils inherent in absolutism. As the theologian Reinhold Niebuhr summed it up, "Man's capacity for justice makes democracy possible, but man's inclination to justice makes democracy necessary."

A second test for leadership is the end for which power is sought. When leaders have as their goal the supremacy of a master race or the promotion of totalitarian revolution or the acquisition and exploitation of colonies or the protection of greed and privilege or the preservation of personal power, it is likely that their leadership will do little to advance the cause of humanity. When their goal is the abolition of slavery, the liberation of women, the enlargement of opportunity for the poor and powerless, the extension of equal rights to racial minorities, the defense of the freedoms of expression and opposition, it is likely that their leadership will increase the sum of human liberty and welfare.

Leaders have done great harm to the world. They have also conferred great benefits. You will find both sorts in this series. Even "good" leaders must be regarded with a certain wariness. Leaders are not demigods; they put on their trousers one leg after another just like ordinary mortals. No leader is infallible, and every leader needs to be reminded of this at regular intervals. Irreverence irritates leaders but is their salvation. Unquestioning submission corrupts leaders and demeans followers. Making a cult of a leader is always a mistake. Fortunately hero worship generates its own antidote. "Every hero," said Emerson, "becomes a bore at last."

The single benefit the great leaders confer is to embolden the rest of us to live according to our own best selves, to be active, insistent, and resolute in affirming our own sense of things. For great leaders attest to the reality of human freedom against the supposed inevitabilities of history. And they attest to the wisdom and power that may lie within the most unlikely of us, which is why Abraham Lincoln remains the supreme example of great leadership. A great leader, said Emerson, exhibits new possibilities to all humanity. "We feed on genius . . . . Great men exist that there may be greater men."

Great leaders, in short, justify themselves by emancipating and empowering their followers. So humanity struggles to master its destiny, remembering with Alexis de Tocqueville: "It is true that around every man a fatal circle is traced beyond which he cannot pass; but within the wide verge of that circle he is powerful and free; as it is with man, so with communities." ■

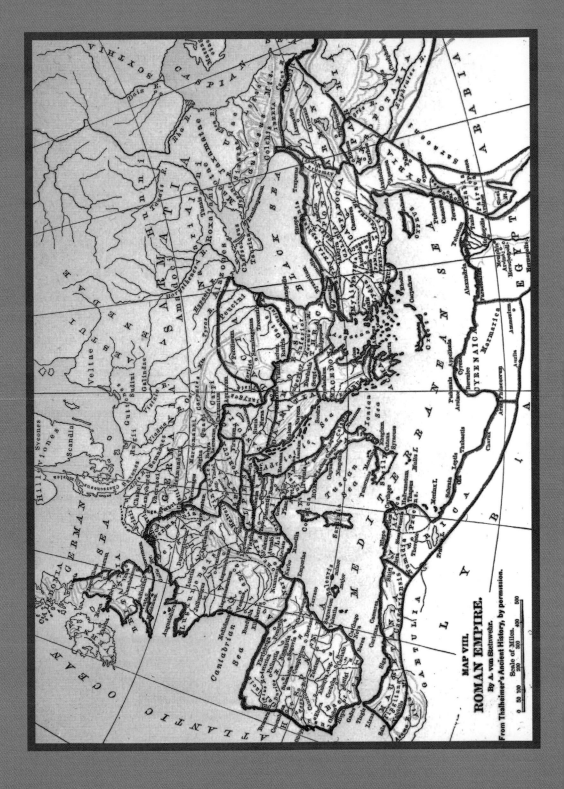

MAP VIII.
ROMAN EMPIRE.
By A. von Steinwehr.

From Thalheimer's Ancient History, by permission.

Scale of Miles.
0 50 100 200 300 400 500

ROMAN YOUTH

Gaius Julius Caesar and his wife Aurelia had a son on July 13, 100 B.C. The Romans knew it as the thirteenth day of the month Quintillus, in the year 653 of the founding of Rome. July thirteenth was also the principal day of the games devoted to the god Apollo. Caesar and Aurelia already had two daughters; this would be their only son. They named the child after his father.

The younger Gaius Julius Caesar grew up in a family that prided itself on being *patrician*—that is, descended from among the early founders of Rome. The family had played a role in Roman politics for centuries. There were also military leaders in the family. The very name "Caesar" came from an ancestor who had killed an elephant in the First Punic War waged between Carthage and Rome.

We know little of Caesar's first ten years. His education was directed by two persons: his mother, Aurelia, and a tutor named Marcus Antonius Ginipho. Ginipho had studied at the city of Alexandria,

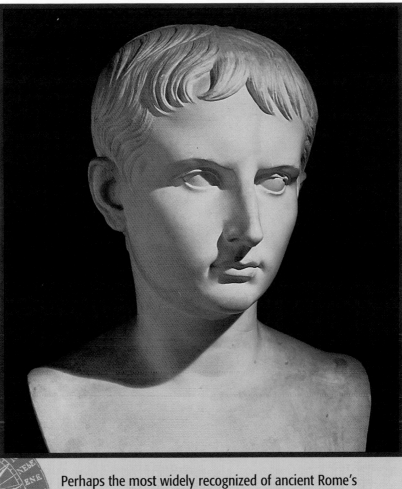

Perhaps the most widely recognized of ancient Rome's many powerful figures, Gaius Julius Caesar transformed a thriving city-state into a fledgling empire, expanding Rome's influence into Gaul and Britain.

Egypt, where he had absorbed much of the great Greek learning we now call "Hellenistic." From an early age, young Caesar knew about the temples and pyramids of Egypt, the city-states and rivalries of the Greeks, and of the heroic conquests of Alexander the Great of Macedon. This early learning appears never to have left him; for the rest of his life, Caesar remained a more worldly and well-read man than most of his political contemporaries. The typical Roman of the time knew a great deal about Rome, its people, and its politics, but Romans were often ignorant about the customs and politics of other lands— but not Caesar. Years later, he would see many of the sites that were described to him by Ginipho.

Aurelia, Caesar's mother, appears to have had a profound influence on the boy. Born in the hilly area north of Rome where the Etruscans had ruled some centuries earlier, Aurelia was less upper-crust than her husband but more ambitious. She "married up" when she married Julius Caesar the Elder, but she generally showed more drive and determination than her husband. Aurelia was a conservative mother in that she raised Caesar to revere the Roman Republic and its grand history. She doubtlessly instilled in him a scorn for most forms of luxury and a desire to prove himself both in politics and in war. This was not unlike the mothers of ancient Sparta, who told their sons as they departed for war: "Come home with your shield [victorious] or on it [dead]."

Caesar's father, Gaius Julius Caesar the Elder, is more of a mystery than his wife. Born into one of the old patrician families, Caesar the Elder did not accomplish a great deal, though he spent many years in political life. He appeared to be on his way to finishing a rather undistinguished career when opportunity came his way—and indeed to the entire Julii family. Caesar's aunt Julia was married to Gaius Marius, then the most powerful man in Rome. Suddenly, when Julius Caesar the Younger was about nine years old, his father had the opportunity to serve Rome in an important capacity.

Marius was the outstanding military leader of his generation. Born in Cereatae, 60 miles southeast of Rome, he was the son of a prosperous farmer, but he was not a patrician. Throughout his long career, Marius was seen as the leader of the Popular (Populares) Party, which was opposed to the Conservative (Senatorial) Party. Marius fought the Gauls, the Germans, and North African tribesmen. Marius also reformed the Roman

Caesar's uncle, Gaius Marius, was the outstanding military leader of his generation. Leader of the Popular Party and a superb general, Marius fought in Gaul, Germany, and North Africa and greatly increased the size and the power of the Roman army.

army, opening it to men who were of age, regardless of their background. Previously, a young man had to be a Roman citizen and own property in order to serve in the legions; Marius changed this and greatly increased the size and the power of the Roman army.

Marius married Julia, a sister of Aurelia, around 112 B.C. Years later, Marius was in early old age, but he commanded Roman armies against those of several Italian city-states in what were called the "Social Wars" of 90–88 B.C. Just before the

Social Wars began, Marius helped to have his brother-in-law, Julius Caesar the Elder, made *praetor* (or governor) of the Roman province of Asia, which really meant a portion of what is now Turkey. Caesar the Elder went east in 91 B.C. In his father's absence, Caesar the Younger began to look upon his uncle Marius as something of a substitute father.

Almost as soon as the Social Wars were concluded, Marius announced he wanted another command. He wanted to go east to fight Mithridates, the King of Pontus, in Asia Minor. Mithridates considered himself a successor to the legacy of Alexander the Great and sought to expand Greek rule throughout the eastern Mediterranean at the cost of Rome.

Marius therefore ran in the elections for *consul* (a top executive position in the Roman government) and won an unprecedented seventh term. He was preparing to go east when a civil war broke out between Marius and Lucius Cornelius Sulla.

Sulla, who had been born in 138 B.C., considered himself the defender of the conservative tradition in Rome. He wanted to deprive Marius of further glory and to be the conqueror of Mithridates. Sulla's men chased Marius and his followers out of Rome, and Sulla went east in 87 B.C. with a large army to chastise the King of Pontus.

Almost as soon as Sulla had departed, Marius and Cinna (his chief colleague) returned to Rome. They carried out a purge of Sulla's supporters and made grand preparations of their own. One aspect of Marius' plans was the further cementing of the relationship between himself and his party and the Julii family. He was already married to Julia. Now he arranged a marriage between Julius Caesar the Younger and Cornelia, who was the daughter of Cinna.

Caesar was willing and ready to marry. He also was able to make his own decisions because his father had died suddenly and unexpectedly, probably of a heart attack. Gaius Julius Caesar was now leader of the Julii family in his own right. It suited his plans and his future ambitions to cement the alliance between the Julii family and the leaders of the Popular Party. He married Cornelia in 85 B.C. They were, by all accounts, a happy and devoted couple.

But tragedy, as the Greeks knew so well, can ruin even the best plans.

Marius died suddenly in 86 B.C. Leadership of his group passed to Cinna. Cinna, however, died while on campaign in Greece in 84 B.C. Suddenly, the Popular Party, as Marius' followers had come to be known, was without a leader. Suddenly, Julius Caesar's boldness in marrying the daughter of Cinna appeared to be a liability.

The day of reckoning came on November 2, 82 B.C. On that frightful day, Caesar, his wife, and indeed all of Rome heard the dreaded words "Sulla *ad portas*! Sulla *ad portas* (Sulla is at the gates)!"

The words *"ad portas"* had a special meaning for most Romans. During the wars between Carthage and Rome, the Carthaginian general Hannibal had once come within sight of the walls of Rome. Though he had never captured the city, Roman mothers still frightened their children into obedience with the words, "Hannibal *ad portas* (Hannibal is at the gates)!"

Sulla had returned from the east, landed his men at Brindisium on the southeast coast of Italy, and marched to Rome. Now the city lay at his feet. Sulla had returned in a vindictive frame of mind. He wanted vengeance for the indignities he had suffered in the past, *and* he wanted to wipe out the leadership of the Popular Party. Therefore, Sulla published a list of those who were proscribed, meaning they were to suffer banishment or death. About 40 Senators and 1,200 knights were eventually put to death under this proscription.

Julius Caesar was on the list. He was, after all, both the nephew of Marius and the son-in-law of Cinna.

Caesar was found and brought before Sulla. The 56-year-old man, who had recently been named Dictator of Rome, frowned at the 18-year-old Julius. Caesar, Sulla announced,

The chief rival of Gaius Marius was General Lucius Cornelius Sulla, defender of the Rome's Conservative Party. As the power struggle between Marius and Sulla raged, Sulla placed his enemies, including a young Julius Caesar, on a death list.

must divorce Cornelia and act as if the marriage had never occurred. Then, and only then, Caesar would be left in peace.

The younger man refused. He refused the most powerful Roman of the day, the first Roman to be made Dictator in nearly 130 years. Perhaps Caesar was inspired by some of the stories told to him by Ginipho of Greek heroes who defied tyrants. Perhaps Caesar was motivated by pride. Perhaps his actions were caused by love. Many other Romans were brought before Sulla and told to divorce their wives who had associations with the Popular Party. Most of them promptly did so.

But Caesar would not. Sulla did not order Caesar's death, but he did confiscate the wealth from Cornelia's family, including all that would have gone to Caesar. Perhaps Sulla hoped that Caesar would change his mind and realign himself with the Conservative Party. If this happened, Caesar could be a valuable asset.

Caesar went into hiding for some time. During the months that he struggled from one cave to another in the hills of central Italy, his relatives made impassioned pleas to Sulla on his behalf. The boy was young, they said. His marriage to Cornelia had been arranged, but now he was in love with her. If Sulla allowed him to live, Caesar might become a valuable Roman in the future. Finally Sulla relented. He did not return the property that had been confiscated, but Caesar's name was removed from the list.

Tradition has it that Sulla remarked to those who pled for Caesar's life, "Keep him since you so wish, but I would have you know that this young man who is so precious to you will one day overthrow the aristocratic party which you and I have fought so hard to defend. There are many Mariuses in him."

Caesar had lived to fight another day. Even Sulla, the most fearsome tyrant of the time, had not been able to tame the lion that lay within Gaius Julius Caesar.

A POLITICAL EDUCATION

The Roman government of 80 B.C. was much the same as it had been 300 years earlier. Rome was proud of, and famous for, her consistency. The Roman government was composed of two executives, a legislature called the Senate, a large number of magistrates, and the Popular Assembly. Two men called *consuls* filled the executive function. Consuls were elected each year by the Senate. The term was for one year, and there were numerous limitations on how old a man had to be to serve as consul, and how many years had to elapse before he could once more run for the office.

There were two consuls, rather than one, because the Romans believed in a balance of power. They had thrown out the last Etruscan King in 509 B.C. and had no wish for future kings. Having two consuls ensured that one man would not dominate the State. Two consuls also meant that one could govern the city of Rome while the other ran the armies in the field. It was a practical division of

Republican Rome was composed of two executives (called *consuls*), a legislature called the *Senate*, a large number of magistrates, and the *Popular Assembly*. The two consuls shared executive authority in the hope that no one leader could seize too much power.

power, and the Romans were an extremely practical people.

Three hundred men made up the *Senate*. The primary qualification to become a *senator* was to have previously served as a magistrate in some capacity. The Senate therefore was made up of men who had political experience. This was a good thing since the Senate ran most of the day-to-day affairs of Rome.

Ten *tribunes* served as a check on the senatorial power.

Long ago, perhaps as early as 400 B.C., the lower classes of Rome, known as *plebeians*, had revolted against the upper classes and demanded a form of redress against the Senate. The upper class had granted the lower class the right to have ten tribunes, who were elected annually by the Popular Assembly.

The ten tribunes sat in the Senate. They did not vote on legislation, but they had an important power which they could exercise by standing up and shouting *Veto* ("I forbid")! By doing this, the tribune could prevent the proposed legislation from going forward. In fact, the Senate was required to immediately cease all discussion on the subject. In this way, the tribunes were supposed to protect the power of the lower classes.

There were a large number of magistrates. The *censors* guarded the public morals. They inspected the streets, kept immoral material out of the public hands, and watched over the attitudes of the Roman people. The *aediles* guarded the treasury. Each aedile had a different section of the treasury that was his responsibility. The *questors* published the news of the government functions and presided over the courts. Even the *Vestal Virgins*, who technically were not magistrates, had important functions. They guarded the public morals, and they held all the wills and deeds of the Roman people.

Finally, at the bottom of this government, was the *Popular Assembly*. From time immemorial, the Assembly had technically held all the power in the Roman State, but as Rome had grown larger and greater, it had been necessary to delegate most of the responsibility to the 300 members of the Senate.

The historian Polybius wrote that if one looked at the consuls and their powers, then Rome would appear to be a monarchy with two heads, rather than one. If one looked at the Senate and its vast powers, then Rome would appear to be an aristocracy, because very few Senators came from other than the top families. And finally, if one looked at the tribunes, their veto power, and the Popular Assembly, then one could only conclude that Rome was truly a Republic.

Rome's strength lay in the diversity of her political institutions. At the root, all the institutions were designed to prevent the rule of one person or one faction. Yet one person, Sulla, had come forward to rule, and he represented one faction—the reactionary members of the Senate.

After he purged Rome of the followers of Marius and Cinna, Sulla relaxed into a form of retirement. He was still the Dictator of Rome, and he continued to watch out for the Conservative interests, but he did not run the day-to-day matters of the city. After 81 B.C., when Sulla had reluctantly spared his life, Caesar spent most of his time in the Kingdom of Bithynia in Asia Minor, waiting for the political winds to change.

Sulla died of natural causes in 78 B.C. Caesar soon returned to Rome and began to play a role in the city's politics. Caesar's first major speech came on the occasion of his aunt Julia's funeral. She was the widow of Marius, and Marius' name had been banned in Rome for the past ten years. Caesar, however, gave a stirring speech in honor of his aunt, and, by implication, in honor of his uncle Marius. Images of Marius were paraded through parts of the city for the first time in ten years. Through this one speech, Caesar showed himself to be a coming man.

Caesar's wife Cornelia died in 68 B.C. Caesar soon married Pompeia, who was a granddaughter of Sulla. The marriage surprised many people who remembered Caesar's previous defiance of Sulla. Caesar had already become a devious and skillful politician, one who could change direction when it suited his cause.

In 63 B.C., Caesar ran for the elected office of Pontifex Maximus ("Chief Priest") of Rome. Many people were offended by Caesar's candidacy. He seemed too young and too worldly to head the Roman religion. Caesar had staked everything on this political contest. Knowing that the office was for life and that it carried great prestige, he ran up enormous debts during the campaign and used every bit of financial and political capital available to him. When he left

Rome's Senate was made up of 300 men with a proven history of political experience. Together, they were responsible for managing most of the day-to-day affairs of Rome.

home on the morning of the election, Caesar told his mother that she would see him either become the Pontifex Maximus or that he would go into exile. Caesar won the vote by a very close margin. He had paid a high price, but it was a position that was held for life, and it became one of the important bases of support upon which he could draw.

One year later, in 62 B.C., scandal struck the home of Julius

Caesar. During the festival of the *Bona Dea* ("Good Goddess"), a minor politician named Clodius snuck into Caesar's house dressed as a woman. This was not unusual, in that Clodius was both a friend of Caesar and an admirer of Caesar's wife Pompeia. The timing was atrocious. The festival of the Bona Dea was celebrated by women only, and Caesar, as the Pontifex Maximus, was careful to observe such rituals. Clodius was first discovered in the house by the watchful eye of Aurelia, Caesar's mother. Unfortunately the story spread rapidly throughout Rome. Soon everyone in the city knew that the home of the Pontifex Maximus had been violated by the presence of a man during the festival. What was worse, many tongues wagged that Caesar was unable to keep his wife content and that she actively sought the advances of Clodius.

Caesar now showed his great ambition and unscrupulous methods. When the news broke and Clodius was brought to trial, people expected Caesar to denounce Clodius as a vile man, but this did not happen. Instead, Caesar was quiet throughout the early stages of the trial. Only when he came to the witness stand did he testify that he had no knowledge of the affair between Clodius and Pompeia. Incredulously, the prosecutor asked, "Why then did you divorce your wife?"

"Because I insist that my wife should be above suspicion," Caesar answered in a nonchalant manner.

The divorce had already taken place. Caesar had acted quietly and effectively to stem the damage to his reputation. The expression "Caesar's wife must be above suspicion" remains an important political saying to this day. Clodius was found innocent (the jurors were bribed) and then became a quiet but effective ally of Caesar.

Soon after the scandal and trial, Caesar went to Spain as the praetor for that province. Caesar had previously served as the questor for Spain; now he returned as the governor and military leader.

We know little about the extent of Caesar's military experience to this point. He had served under the King of Bithynia, and he had shown his alacrity in the way he handled a group of pirates who had captured him in the eastern Mediterranean. None of these early commands, however, had been enough to show whether Caesar was a true army man, or if he was, like many Roman nobles, only to spend a short time in the military before using that career to springboard into politics.

Now Caesar showed his critics that he was no amateur. Almost at once upon his arrival in Spain, Caesar announced the creation of a new legion: the Tenth Legion. Until about twenty years earlier, legions could only be created by the Senate and Popular Assembly. During the time of Sulla and afterward, victorious generals like Pompey had started the new precedent of creating legions, and then having them confirmed by a vote in the Senate. Caesar thus continued this tradition. The new Tenth Legion was added to the other two already stationed in the province. The new Tenth Legionnaires were young men, predominantly Spanish. As a gesture to please them, Caesar gave the legion the bull as its emblem (bulls were popular in Spain, even then).

Caesar then moved against the tribes of eastern Spain. Coastal Spain, along the Mediterranean, had been conquered by Rome nearly 100 years earlier, but inland Spain, extending to the Atlantic Ocean, was still the realm of the Iberian tribesmen. Caesar marched against the tribes, attacking, capturing, and often burning their towns. Though his praetorship extended for only one year, Caesar did much to extend Roman control throughout Spain. By the time he left for Rome, he had enhanced his military reputation and had gained the unswerving allegiance of the men of the Tenth Legion. It was said that he remembered the names of all his centurions, and that he could call upon them to undertake special tasks on his behalf.

Caesar's victories over the Iberian tribesmen were little reported in Rome. Therefore, when Caesar returned to Rome in 60 B.C., he was still considered something of a political light-weight: handsome, charming, gifted with the populace, but not a major player or formidable opponent. Caesar showed his political skill clearly on his return. He had submitted his name for consul for the year 60 B.C. He knew, as all Romans did, that a consul was not allowed to have a military triumph within the city limits. Therefore he was faced with a difficult choice: whether to be consul or to have the adulation of the crowd.

As it turned out, this was an easy decision for Caesar to make. He wanted and needed to be consul. A triumph was a secondary matter.

As events turned out, it was a fortunate time for Caesar to have returned to Rome at this time. There was a situation that called for someone with a silver tongue, a large purse, and mighty ambitions.

3

THE GREAT TRIUMVIRATE

At the age of 39, Julius Caesar had achieved things that were considerable, but not great. Due to his charm, wealth, and free-spending habits, he had acquired more friends than enemies. His position as Pontifex Maximus placed him constantly in the eye of the Roman crowd. To make the most of his chances, though, Caesar had to find allies. Caesar knew this when he returned to Rome; so did those in the Senate who wanted to prevent Caesar's continued rise in politics. Had he chosen an obvious path, his foes might have thwarted him, but Caesar took on what seemed like a hopeless and thankless task: to bring together Gaius Pompey and Marcus Crassus.

Born in 106 B.C., Pompey was from a distinguished Roman family. Early in life he had caught the eye and attention of Sulla, who had entrusted important military commands to him.

In 67 B.C., the Senate decided to free the Mediterranean from

Gaius Pompeius Magnus (Pompey the Great) was a skilled military leader. He not only rid the Mediterranean of pirates who threatened Roman shipping, but also defeated King Mithridates of Pontus, who had so far repelled all Roman efforts to overthrow him.

the hosts of pirates who seized ships and held wealthy Romans —like the young Caesar—for ransom. The command was given to Pompey. So great was the public trust that Pompey was given the honor of *imperium* (supreme command) not only on the waters of the Mediterranean but up to 60 miles inland if he needed to pursue the pirates to their lairs. Technically this gave Pompey the ability to bring soldiers right to Rome itself, but this was overlooked in the need to bring an end to the pirate menace.

At the height of his powers and prestige, Pompey rid the Mediterranean of its pirates in a lightning-quick campaign of six months. He organized convoys with military galleys that thwarted pirate attacks; he hunted down pirates in their island lairs; and sometimes he pursued them inland. Half a year after he began, Pompey had won the most complete victory at sea that his fellow Romans could have imagined.

The victory over the pirates was but the beginning. Pompey went to the eastern Mediterranean to fight Mithridates, the King of Pontus. This was the same Mithridates against whom Sulla had fought years earlier. During the course of a long reign, Mithridates had fought three separate wars against Rome. Never had Mithridates succeeded in his grand ambitions, but neither had Rome been able to overthrow him. Now Pompey went against Mithridates.

One Roman general after another had failed to subdue Mithridates, but Pompey succeeded. Pompey was known for his thorough command of logistics and careful planning. He organized campaigns that succeeded because supplies arrived on time, and detachments went where they were supposed to go. All of this was masterminded by Pompey. Mithridates was defeated. He died soon after of natural causes, and his body was brought before Pompey as a sign of submission. The son, Pharnaces, who brought the body, will appear again in our story of Caesar and Rome.

After he defeated Mithridates, Pompey went on further military excursions that can really be called adventures. There was no need, strictly speaking, for Pompey to enter Phoenicia and Judea; he did so because these were lands full of fable and, perhaps, of riches. These lands at the eastern end of the

King Mithridates was a savvy military leader who had fought many Roman generals (including Sulla) to a draw. Pompey, however, used superb planning and organization to defeat Mithridates, who died soon after of natural causes.

Mediterranean never knew a Roman conqueror until Pompey; he was the first Roman to besiege Jerusalem, and the first to enter the holy Temple which was built by King Solomon, destroyed by the Babylonians, and then rebuilt about 520 B.C. Perhaps out of superstitious fear, Pompey left the Temple treasures where they were instead of taking them for himself or in the name of the Roman People.

Additionally, Pompey continued on minor campaigns in the Middle East and reached nearly as far as the Caspian Sea. When he returned to Rome in 78 B.C., Pompey was one of the most traveled of all Romans and was certainly the most renowned.

Pompey returned to Rome in 61 B.C. His foes feared he would come as Sulla had before him, to initiate a reign of iron and blood. But Pompey proved remarkably moderate—perhaps even naive. He disbanded his forces when he landed at Brindisum on Italy's southeast coast and marched to Rome with only a handful of comrades. Pompey presented himself to the Senate as the most successful conqueror Rome had seen in 100 years, and as one of the few who was able to resist the temptation to take over the government. However, he was not rewarded for this. The Senate ignored Pompey to the extent that it could and refused to ratify the promises he had made to his soldiers concerning land grants.

Pompey was furious. To whom he could turn? Certainly not to Marcus Licinius Crassus. He and Pompey were old rivals, whose rivalry had gone over the line to bitter hatred.

Born in 110 B.C., Marcus Crassus came from one of the noblest and most distinguished of all Roman families. Unlike Caesar, who wore his dignity lightly, and who worked to please the Roman crowd, Crassus had a deep and abiding dislike of the common people. He believed it was his right, indeed his mission, to further the cause of aristocratic government, and down deep he despised the type of compromises made by ambitious men like Caesar.

Like Pompey, Crassus had risen because he had caught the attention of Sulla. Crassus and Sulla were very much alike; both of them believed in the rule of the patricians, and both scorned to win the favor of the populace. For these reasons, one might expect that Sulla would favor Crassus. In most cases, Sulla appeared to prefer the services of Pompey, and he would sometimes condescendingly compare Crassus' accomplishments to Pompey's. One of Crassus' most bitter memories revolved around the crisis that had been caused by the slave rebellion led by Spartacus. Crassus had been the Roman who had risen to the occasion. He had received extraordinary powers from the Senate, had mobilized the army, and had won critical victories over Spartacus toward the rebellion's end. For all this, however, Crassus received much less attention than did Pompey, who had had the good fortune to return to Italy in time to play an important last-minute role. Rather than remember Crassus as their savior, the people of Rome turned to Pompey as their hero.

There was one area, though, in which Crassus had no equal. He was a master at making money. During the years he had been one of Sulla's henchmen, Crassus had perfected certain financial techniques. Later, when he struck out on his own, Crassus developed Rome's first fire department. It was not a true municipal service; the department belonged entirely to Crassus. As the years went on, Crassus developed a technique which made him the wealthiest man in Rome. When an alarm sounded, Crassus and his fire engines hastened to the scene of the fire. There, Crassus would make a very low offer to the owner of the home that was burning. Should the homeowner indignantly refuse, Crassus would simply stand by, and the fire engines did the same. But once the owner agreed to sell, nearly always for a rock bottom price, then Crassus would send the engines to work. In this way he became the single greatest owner of real estate within the city.

Crassus' wealth made him the subject of envy, jokes, and downright anger. He used the money to many purposes, not the least of which was to become the bankroller for the political campaigns of many of his colleagues. Nearly everyone who mattered in Rome, it was said, owed money to Crassus.

Crassus was about 55 years old in 60 B.C. The years had brought him great wealth and influence, but little fame. He

Although under-celebrated as a military leader, Crassus (right) was skilled at making money and was one of the wealthiest men in Rome. Crassus and Pompey were bitter rivals until Caesar applied his flattery and persuasion to the situation, reconciling the two men and gaining more power for himself.

ached for a military command with which he could outshine Pompey. The rivalry between the two men had only increased over the years, and Crassus was eager to find a way to bring Pompey down to earth. Therefore, when Julius Caesar came with propositions, Crassus was willing to listen.

Pompey too, was willing to entertain ideas from Caesar. Pompey already regretted his magnanimous gesture in disbanding his troops at Brindisium. If he had them in Rome now, the Senate would not be able to ignore his demands.

Caesar called upon both Pompey and Crassus by turns. He flattered each of them, told them they were the most important Romans of their generation, and that it was shameful that Rome failed to honor them properly. Then Caesar made his proposition. Rather than continue to vie with one another, Pompey and Crassus should join him and form a three-way political partnership. Pompey would provide the military brilliance and the popularity with his men; Crassus had the wealth and the respect of the conservative Senators; and he, Caesar, was beloved by the Roman crowd. Together they would harness the energies of the military, the finances, and the popular will. They would become what has been called ever since the First Triumvirate (it was "first" because Octavian, Mark Antony, and Lepidus formed another one 30 years later).

Only someone like Caesar could have pulled this off. Somehow, he brought Pompey, Crassus, and himself together into an alliance that was able to defy the Senate.

Caesar was doing so much for Pompey, for Crassus, and for the good of the state. What was he getting for himself? Plenty, as it turned out. Caesar was named consul for the year 59 B.C. and granted proconsular power in not one but two provinces, Cisalpine Gaul and Transalpine Gaul. (Cisalpine Gaul was what is now northern Italy, and Transalpine Gaul was what is now southern France.) Anyone who previously had thought Caesar lacked military ambition now knew such an idea was mistaken. Rather, Caesar was trying to set up a base for conquests that might eventually rival those of Pompey. Pompey appeared willing to take the risk because he needed Caesar's support to make sure the land bill got through the Senate.

Now the howls of discontent arose in the Senate. Finding themselves outmaneuvered, the Senators first tried to block Caesar's consulship and then Pompey's land program for his veterans. The historian Plutarch narrates the response of the three men who formed the new Triumvirate:

> And so Caesar was escorted to the consulship, protected and surrounded by the friendship of Crassus and Pompey. He was elected with a clear majority, with Calpurnius Bibulus as his colleague, and as soon as he took up the post he began to introduce the kind of proposals for allotments and grants of land, designed to please the masses, that one might have expected from the most radical of tribunes, but not from a consul.

Tribunes were expected to safeguard the interests of the common people. Consuls were expected to lead the state in military matters and to work for the interests of the patricians.

When the Senate balked at the proposals, Caesar went before the people in the Popular Assembly. With Pompey on his right side and Crassus on his left, Caesar proclaimed the necessity of the new laws. Pompey threatened to back them up with sword and shield. Crassus made no public declaration, but everyone knew he was at one with Caesar and Pompey. Conservative Senators ground their teeth, but the bills were passed.

There was one last piece of business. In 60 B.C., Caesar married his daughter Julia to Pompey. It was designed to weld the two men close together and to prevent treacherous acts by either while Caesar was away from Rome. Pompey was nearly 30 years older than his new bride, but it became, by all accounts, a happy marriage. Some historians even suggest that Pompey's ambition began to ebb at this time, and that he savored the pleasures of home life more than the struggles of political life.

This was Caesar's last season in Rome for many years. He left the great city in January 59 B.C., and headed northward over the Alps to Gaul. Caesar, the glamorous youth, had become Caesar the skillful politician. Would he now acquit himself as well on the battlefield?

CAESAR
IN GAUL

When Caesar arrived in Cisalpine Gaul, he found the Roman legions there in a high state of readiness. These were troops who had to be so ready that they could be dispatched at a day's notice to serve in the Alps or beyond. Even more important, they were the last major body of soldiers between Rome and her foes to the north. The Romans never forgot that Gallic tribesmen had come south in 390 B.C. and laid waste to the city of Rome.

No one expected great things from the new consul. Caesar was into middle age, and previous leaders—such as Marius and Pompey—had gained great laurels by the time they were thirty. Caesar was known as a fine speaker (his training at Rhodes had been beneficial) and an excellent diplomat, but not a battlefield commander. It was expected that Caesar would at most hold the line against the Gauls and Germans to the north.

A Roman legionnaire. Caesar helped refine the capabilities of the Roman legions, using catapults and battering rams to conquer Gaul (an area now occupied by northern Italy and southern France).

The men whom Caesar now commanded were drawn from the best Roman legions, soldiers who followed a military tradition that had been honed to perfection over about 200 years. Rome had developed the legion, a mobile division of 6,000 men, that had proved superior to the Greek phalanx. Each legion was broken down into groups called *maniples* and *centuries*, each of which was commanded by a *centurion*. The commander of 100 men, the centurion was considered the backbone of the Roman military machine.

The Romans had seized upon and improved techniques of siege warfare, including the use of catapults and battering rams. They had also learned to create night camps that were practically forts of their own. Every Roman legionnaire (soldier) carried a shovel as well as his short sword. A Roman legion could stop marching at five in the afternoon and have a trench dug with small fortifications put up by nine that evening. This backbreaking labor prevented the types of ambushes and night attacks for which Rome's enemies were famous.

The single best source for Caesar's campaigns in the north is his own *Commentaries*, published around 50 B.C. Generations of students—both Romans and then Europeans, and finally Americans—learned the first few words of the *Commentaries* by heart:

> All Gaul is divided in three parts. They are inhabited respectively by the Belgae, the Aquitani, and a people who call themselves Celts, though we call them Gauls. All of these have different languages, customs, and laws. The Celts are separated from the Aquitani by the river Garonne, from the Belgae by the Marne and Seine. The Belgae are the bravest of the three peoples, being farthest removed from the highly developed civilization of the Roman Province, least often visited by merchants with enervating luxuries for sale, and nearest to the Germans across the Rhine, with whom they are continually at war.

The areas which Caesar described encompass most of modern France and Belgium. The division between the Aquitani and Gauls, which he places at the Garonne River, remains an important linguistic and cultural divide today.

What Caesar describes as the "Roman Province" was in the very south of France. Today it is called Provence and is known for its hot weather and beautiful beaches.

Caesar found a crisis in Transalpine Gaul in the spring of 59 B.C. The Helvetti, a Gallic tribe located in what is now Switzerland, wanted to migrate south and west through the Roman Province. The Helvetti were hemmed in by the lack of room in their homeland and needed to migrate to find better lands. At another time, and under the command of another leader, the Romans might have allowed this migration. Julius Caesar knew that to allow one such movement would encourage others to follow. Therefore, he demanded that the Helvetti return to their ancestral lands.

The Helvetti tried to cross the Rhone River, which flows from north to south and empties into the Mediterranean. They found Caesar's men watching the fords, and even the use of boats was to no avail. Caesar had stopped the Helvetti just in time. The tribesmen turned and moved as if to return to their native area, but Caesar followed them; he wanted to be sure they would not change their minds. The Helvetti leaders sent diplomats to Caesar, urging him to leave them alone, but he continued to pursue.

About two months after the Helvetti first began their march and about one month after they began their retreat, Caesar fought a great pitched battle against them. The fight was close in many respects, and there were moments when it became desperate for sections of Caesar's army. At the crucial moments, however, Roman discipline and Roman organization prevailed. The centurions could manage their centuries in a way that no Gallic or German tribal leader could, and by the end of the day, the Helvetti were flying in full retreat. Caesar later wrote that some 380,000 Helvetti began the march of migration, and that only 110,000 of these ever returned home. This is almost certainly an exaggeration, but given that Caesar's *Commentaries* is the only history that

Gaul was not a single nation, but three distinct regions, each with its own tribal chieftains, customs, and language. Caesar knew that gaining victory in Gaul would mean fighting each of these groups separately using well-coordinated Roman troops. Shown here is a Gallic tribesman.

survives, one can surmise that he did inflict a great defeat, and that many thousands of the Helvetti were killed.

To say that Rome was surprised would be an understatement. Caesar, the darling of the crowds, the elegant nobleman, had shown himself to be a great general. Just as important, he was ruthless in a way that the Senate and Roman people could appreciate.

A few weeks after his great victory over the Helvetii, Caesar learned of a new, pressing danger. This time it was German tribesmen, led by a king named Ariovistus.

The Germanic tribesmen were distantly related to the Gauls, but there the comparison ended. The Germans were known for being much fiercer and more warlike than the Gauls, and recent incursions into Gaul had shown the Germans how fertile the soil there was. Ariovistus was one of a number of Germanic leaders who claimed the right to sections on the west bank of the Rhine River; now he made his move.

Ordinarily the Gauls would have fought the Germans on their own. Many Gallic leaders, especially their Druidic priests, told the people that if they relied on the Romans, they would end up with a new set of invaders and conquerors. The Gauls were spent from a long series of internal wars between the tribes of Audea and those led by Arverni. Given this weakness, many Gauls solicited Caesar and asked him to stop the German invasion. Naturally, Caesar was only too happy to oblige.

Caesar marched rapidly and confronted Ariovistus on the west side of the Rhine River, perhaps near the border of present-day Switzerland and Germany. The German king was astounded that Caesar had moved so far so quickly, and he asked for peace negotiations. The talks that followed were more a form of sparring between the two leaders than a genuine hope for peace. Ariovistus explained that his people needed more land, for their herds of horses and cattle. Caesar agreed that this was true, but declared the Germans could not enter Gaul, which, he said, was under his protection. Many Gallic tribesmen were happy to hear this at the time, but they did not realize the extent to which Caesar would later use this claim against them.

So the issue would be resolved by force of arms. The Germans had crossed the Rhine in a state of high confidence, but Caesar's quick movements had taken them aback, and they now assumed a defensive posture. Ariovistus brought out his men and aligned the groups according to their tribal heritage: Harudes, Marcomanni, Triboci, Vangiones, Nemetes, Eudusii. Caesar correctly perceived that these tribal divisions were a weakness that he might exploit. The Germans, like the Gauls, fought tribe for tribe, and even man for man, so that they might receive personal acclaim for their deeds. By contrast, Caesar's legionnaires fought as one compact, mass unit. The day that Caesar met Ariovistus was probably the largest clash between two such different military systems since Crassus had defeated Spartacus 15 years earlier.

Caesar began the battle with a charge by his front lines. The Germans at once were thrown on the defensive, and they adopted their shield wall technique that had often worked for them in the past. But many Romans actually jumped on top of the wall of shields and hacked their way downward, causing consternation in the German lines.

Within just a few hours it was all over. The Germans who escaped the battle fled north and west, headed for the Rhine. Ariovistus and a handful of followers found rafts and made their way across to safety. But his army was completely shattered, and the women and children the Germans had brought with them were taken captive; most were later sold into slavery. Like many other Roman commanders, Caesar was an active participant in the slave trade. Thousands upon thousands of the captives from his campaigns were sold in slave markets around the Mediterranean, helping to make Caesar a very wealthy man.

Once again, Rome was astounded to learn of another great victory by Caesar. The Senate voted for several days of thanksgiving, and special tokens of honor were sent to Caesar.

The following spring Caesar marched against the tribes collectively known as the Belgae. The modern-day nation of Belgium takes its name from these tribes, who lived between the Sambre and Rhine rivers. Caesar described them in his

Commentaries as the most warlike of the tribes of Gaul, because of their proximity to the Germans with whom they often fought. Some of the German customs infiltrated into the Belgae as well; the Belgae were the only tribes in Gaul that practiced cremation, a German custom.

Caesar moved against the Belgae, claiming that they had amassed a great army to fight him. Because the Belgae left no written records, it is difficult to say whether they were indeed the aggressors, but as usual, Caesar's speed of movement allowed them no opportunity to take advantage. Caesar was soon crossing the first rivers into their lands.

The area controlled by the Belgae was wetter and swampier than it is today (the dams built by the Dutch over the last thousand years have vastly changed the terrain for the better). The Rhine River splits into many different channels as it nears the North Sea, creating a bewildering mass of water and swampy land. Amidst these channels and rivulets, the Belgae awaited Caesar's advance.

Several of the Belgae tribes yielded as soon as Caesar arrived. He followed the usual custom of demanding hostages to ensure their good behavior, but he soon pushed on because he learned that the Nervii, the most warlike of the Belgae, had gathered a great force of 60,000 warriors.

The battles that followed were a series of close-runs. Caesar had the advantage of his soldiers' discipline and his own decisive leadership; the Nervii had the advantage of the terrain, and their own fanatical (according to Caesar) willingness to resist. In the last battle, Caesar was in serious trouble. The Nervii commanded a river bank, and Caesar and two of his legions were pinned down at the water's edge. The historian Plutarch claims that all was lost until Caesar seized the shield of a dead centurion and, wearing his traditional scarlet cloak, inspired his men with his own courage. The legion that had been hanging back in reserve now came forward with speed, and Caesar won yet another resounding victory.

Caesar used the speed of his legions to out-maneuver the Gallic tribesmen, and in the end brought victory to Rome. Here, a Gallic princess offers wine to her Roman conquerors.

Completely chastened, the Nervii came forward in submission. Caesar took numerous hostages, but he probably knew that this foe would not oppose him again; he had done too much damage to the Nervii. And so, within two years of coming to Gaul, Caesar had defeated the Helvetti, Ariovistus the German, and the tribes of the Belgae. He had fought on the Alsatian plain, near the mountain passes of Switzerland,

and in the swampy marshes of what is now Belgium. Caesar's accomplishments were all the more remarkable considering the different opponents he faced and the different terrain on which he fought. He had become a general of the first rank, and the only Roman who now could compare to him was Gaius Pompey.

How does one account for Caesar's remarkable success? Here was a man who had never commanded in the field until his late thirties, and who had always seemed better at pleasing the crowds than at command. What was his secret?

First, Caesar was extremely ambitious. Even during the times when he appeared to be absorbed in social activities, Caesar was always reading, always planning. Second, Caesar inherited a northern army that had been brought to the peak of its success under the command of Marius 40 years earlier. Caesar did not have to invent the legion, the maniple, the *cohort* (a unit of 600 men), or the *gladius* (short sword). All these were in place by the time he became the commander of Transalpine Gaul.

Perhaps even more important was the army's speed. Caesar never waited for his enemies; he consistently moved faster than his foes. Against another traditional army, as perhaps against the Greeks or Parthians, this would not have been so important, but the mixed tribal groups of Gauls and Germans that Caesar fought were consistently astonished by the speed of his movements.

Julius Caesar was now a force known from Rome to the Atlantic Ocean. Though they might have pronounced his name differently, the Gallic, Germanic, and even British tribes knew that the man in the scarlet cloak was one of the most devastating war leaders ever seen.

5

CAESAR IN GERMANY AND BRITAIN

C aesar made it a practice to return to Cisalpine Gaul every winter, leaving his troops in their camps in Gaul. He wanted to be close to Rome, to keep a sounding of which way the political winds blew. By the winter of 56–55 B.C., Caesar knew that events were reaching a dangerous point.

Caesar's incredible successes in Gaul had earned him many enemies at home. The common people of Rome still cheered his name, but many Senators, especially those who remembered the dire prediction made by Sulla, now thought of Caesar as the worst of enemies. He combined the military skill of Marius with the political skill that was all his own.

So long as Crassus and Pompey did their part to keep Rome calm, Caesar had little to worry about. But the First Triumvirate was already beginning to show signs of strain. Crassus was displeased by the lack of attention to all his services to Rome; Pompey appeared to be in

After his decisive victory in Gaul, Caesar turned his attentions to the island of Britain. Caesar's first invasion attempt was thwarted, however, when ships supplying grain to the Roman legions were blown off course by a storm.

something of a daze. Though he had been an amazing leader in the field and on the sea against the pirates, Pompey seemed at a loss when it came to Roman politics. Rather than lead and develop a strong "Pompey" faction—or even a "Pompey, Crassus and Caesar" faction—Pompey drifted, sometimes taking the advice of a certain group of Senators and sometimes others.

Caesar met his colleagues at Luculla in 55 B.C. Whether or not they still liked each other, the three men committed to another five years of working together. Caesar received his prize; his command in Gaul was extended by another five years. Pompey received command of Roman forces in Spain, and Crassus was granted command of an ambitious expedition against the Parthians, who inhabited the land between the Tigris and Euphrates rivers in what is modern-day Iraq. With matters settled between him and his colleagues, Caesar hastened northward to Gaul.

Caesar had ambitious plans for the upcoming campaign season. Until now, Caesar had been forced to respond to the invasions of the Helvetti and German tribes. Though he had beaten them soundly, it was they who chose when to cross the Rhine River and to invade Gaul. Caesar had been forced to react, rather than to initiate events. That would now change.

Sometime in the early summer of 55 B.C., Caesar approached the Rhine at one of its narrower parts, perhaps near the present-day city of Coblenz, Germany. The German tribes never bothered to defend the right bank of the Rhine. They considered this completely unnecessary, since their neighbors cowered in fear of them, rather than the other way around. Thus there were no German forces on either side of the Rhine.

Caesar had his men start to build a bridge. Romans were excellent builders and engineers, but this was a mighty task because of the swiftness of the current and the depth of the riverbed. The first few efforts all came to naught, but then Caesar's men began to experiment with laying "piles" in the riverbed. Piles, which have been used by engineers ever since, allow a firm, though usually temporary, foundation on which bridges can be built. The piles were made of large planks of wood; there was no lack of wood in the vicinity. Then, on top of the piles, Caesar's men laid wooden planks, knotted together with rope. Within 18 days the bridge was complete, and Caesar and his army marched east over the Rhine. As simple as those words sound today, this was the first time it had been done— previously the Germans always used rafts or simply swam across the great river.

The Germanic tribesmen simply were not ready for Caesar. After he crossed the Rhine, Caesar marched steadily eastward for several days. His progress was slow, because the area was heavily forested (parts of the forest, known as the Black Forest, remain today). Wherever he went, Caesar found that the Germans avoided battle; they fled their towns and dispersed into the woods. This was not at all disappointing to Caesar, for the German reluctance to fight allowed for an easy march with few casualties. The Germans melted away, and Caesar's progress on the eastern side of the Rhine was more like a triumphal procession than a true campaign.

After two weeks, Caesar returned to the Rhine. His army crossed over, and Caesar destroyed the bridge, rather than leave it as an easy road for the Germans to use. He built a strong fort on the west bank of the Rhine and left enough men to ensure that the Germans would know of their presence. Then he headed due west to the waters we call the English Channel today, with the intent to conquer Britain. In his *Commentaries*, Caesar made it sound as if he decided to cross the Channel just after he crossed the Rhine. Historians, who know the complexities of the invasion, are certain that Caesar must have begun planning the Channel crossing months before, and that his lieutenants on the coast of Gaul must have been procuring ships and boats all that spring and early summer.

Caesar assembled his men at the Gallic port town of Gesoriacum, which is present-day Bolougne, on the coast of Normandy in France. Caesar gave it a new name, Portus Itius. There he assembled about 10,000 men in 30 ships. While he awaited a favorable wind and tide, Caesar sent one of his

Knowing that the Germans had left the eastern bank of the Rhine River undefended, Caesar ordered the construction of a bridge at one of the river's narrowest points, thus enabling him to guide his legions easily into Germany. Here Romans destroy German huts.

most favored tribunes, named Volusenus, to reconnoiter the British coast. Volusensus was perhaps the first Roman to see the white cliffs of Dover. He went further and saw the beginnings of shale beaches where Caesar might land. Volusensus returned and gave the news to Caesar, who embarked with his expeditionary force around midnight on August 25, 55 B.C. This departure time sounds strange to us today, but Caesar was making the most of the wind and tide to get out of the harbor at Portus Itius (William the Conqueror would also use an early evening departure time when he invaded Britain more than 1,110 years later).

Late August of 55 B.C. brought blustery weather to the waters between Britain and Gaul. Early autumn was not an auspicious time to cross the waters to Britain, but Julius Caesar seldom backed away from any challenge. He had learned in years of fighting the Gauls and the Germans that decision and speed were among the most important tools in the art of war. Now he brought those tools and his own fearsome reputation across the thirty miles that separated Britain from Gaul. He intended to conquer Britain for Rome.

Historians have ever since debated Caesar's embarkation point. Was it Boulougne in what is now Normandy? Or was it at the Pas-de-Calais, the departure point for the shortest crossing of the Channel? We cannot say for sure, but we are confident that after Caesar and his men departed at midnight, early morning found him in front of the cliffs of Dover, on the southeast side of Britain.

However, the British tribesmen had been alerted and were ready for Caesar. They stood on the white cliffs of Dover and made a menacing sight, brandishing their javelins and making great cries of dread to their enemies. But Caesar had faced many such foes—none were more ferocious than the German tribesmen whom he had recently beaten—and now he planned his landing. It would be foolhardy to set down on the narrow beach and receive the British assault; far better to sail north in search of a better landing spot. Caesar had found his new spot by the next day—a much wider, more open beach without the added danger of cliffs.

One day later the Romans found a beach full of small stones or shingles. The Britons had followed by land, and they came down to the water's edge to oppose the landing. The Romans were the most disciplined and organized soldiers of their day, but they were accustomed to land battles, not to this type of amphibious operation. As the first Romans came ashore they were met by hundreds of Britons, throwing javelins and using occasional chariot charges to disrupt the enemy. For the first hour there was no success in getting ashore, and many Romans were killed or wounded.

A turning point came when a standard bearer inspired his fellow Romans. The man who carried the eagle of the Tenth Legion cried out, "Jump down, comrades, unless you want to surrender our eagle to the enemy. I, at any rate, mean to do my duty to my country and my general." After those words, he leapt into the sea and was one of the first Romans to get a foothold on the beach.

Within an hour, most of the Roman landing force had made it ashore. The Britons fell back in disarray; Caesar's first amphibious landing had been carried out. It was a heady ending to what had been an eventful day. Once ashore, Caesar and his Roman legionnaires utilized their shovels and began making a fortified camp. Within one day, Caesar had a fortified camp in place, and from this position he was virtually invincible.

The Britons had already entertained doubts about the wisdom of resisting Caesar. British emissaries entered Caesar's camp on the third day of his arrival and asked for peace. Caesar was initially harsh toward the emissaries, but then accepted their pleas; he also accepted a number of hostages to ensure the good behavior of their fellows. The invasion of Britain was going splendidly, and then to top things off Caesar learned that the transport ships bearing cargoes of grain had been sighted.

It was the night of the full moon, probably August 31, 55 B.C. Caesar and many of his men watched with eager anticipation as the transport ships appeared and neared the coast. Just minutes before some of the transports would have landed, a contrary wind blew up, and the ships were blown south by southeast, away from the men who anticipated their arrival. The squall turned into a genuine storm, and the tides, heightened by the full moon, carried the ships far off course. Several were wrecked; others limped back to Gaul. It was a naval disaster.

Caesar's second invasion of Britain was not much more successful than his first, but he was able to maintain popular support through skillfully worded letters home.

During his many campaigns in Gaul, Caesar had become famous for his ability to have his men live off the land. The Romans were expert at passing through an area and confiscating the grain and wine they needed. But here in Britain, Caesar had no maps and no trusty guides, and thus did not know where food supplies could be found. The transport ships were therefore extremely important, and their failure to reach the landing spot was a disaster for Caesar's plans.

The Britons appeared to sense Caesar's plight. Just one day after the naval calamity, a group of Romans were caught by Britons while foraging. The Britons made numerous attacks, both with javelins and with men in chariots, and they might have eliminated the Roman cohort had Caesar not arrived with reinforcements. Caesar inflicted a punishing defeat on the Britons in the area, but then withdrew to his beachhead. Even Caesar knew that the omens, the gods, and the season were now against him.

A few days later Caesar re-embarked his army. The Roman ships, piloted by Gallic sailors, went back to Gaul. Caesar's great reconnaissance was something of a failure; he had not penetrated inland and he knew little more about the island than when he had begun. It was in Caesar's nature to learn from his mistakes, and when he returned one year later he would be more dangerous than ever to the men of Britain. Caesar cast a parting shot at these tribesmen in his *Commentaries.* "By far," wrote Caesar, "the most civilized inhabitants are those living in Kent (a purely maritime district), whose way of life differs little from that of the Gauls. Most of the tribes in the interior do not grow corn but live on milk and meat, and wear skins. All the Britons dye their bodies with wood, which produces a blue colour, and shave the whole of their bodies except the head and the upper lip."

Caesar would be back. He never let an initial reverse frighten him off from an action.

When Caesar returned to Portus Itius (Bolougne), he immediately began to prepare for a second invasion of Britain. Caesar had his men gather Gallic carpenters and build ships and boats for the coming year. Caesar then left Gaul and spent the winter in Cisalpine Gaul, as usual. He did not return to

Rome, but the news of his British adventure traveled rapidly and the Roman Senate ordered a thanksgiving session of 20 days to commemorate the event. Some have cast doubt on the Senate's sincerity, but one of the best historians of early Britain affirms that "No one who is versed in Roman literature and gifted with historical imagination will regard the decree as ironical. For Caesar's countrymen may well have felt that he had opened the way for the conquest of a new world."

The new year brought opportunities for all three members of the Triumvirate. Pompey remained in Rome even though he had been made consul for Spain. Crassus went east to take up his governorship of Roman Syria. Because of his immense private wealth, Crassus was able to foot the cost of outfitting more men and legions than would otherwise have been possible. Caesar returned north, eager to do more than he had in 55 B.C.

Caesar's lieutenants in Gaul had done their work well during the winter and spring. By the time Caesar arrived on the coast, he found hundreds of ships built and hundreds more still under construction. Most important from Caesar's viewpoint was that many of the ships could carry horses. Caesar felt that the lack of cavalry had hampered his campaign the previous year.

It was about the tenth of July that Caesar and 30,000 men embarked at Portus Itius. It was close to the time of his birthday, and Caesar was 46 years old. He had come a long way from the aristocratic dandy who had been captured by pirates, and he was determined to go even further. This second invasion of Britain was intended to make his name; he had already secured his fortune through the loot and slaves obtained in Gaul.

THE CONFEDERACY OF VERCINGETORIX

Caesar's second invasion of Britain was not much more success-ful than the first. However, Caesar exaggerated his efforts in his letters to the Senate, and he once again received the applause of the Roman people (the actual conquest of Britain would be accomplished by the Emperor Claudius, in 50 A.D.).

Meanwhile, things changed on the home front. Caesar's appeal to the Roman people remained very high, but his grip on Roman politics was about to slip. The Triumvirate had endured rather well for five years, but it was about to be reduced to the rule of two men. Marcus Crassus died on campaign against Parthia in 54 B.C. Crassus, who long ago had defeated Spartacus and put down the slave rebellion, fell prey to the steppe conditions of Mesopotamia and to his own eagerness for more military glory. Suddenly there was no longer a Triumvirate. Power was now divided between two men: Pompey and Caesar.

Due to his heroic efforts and skill in battle, the Arvernian leader Vercingetorix remains an important symbol of strength to this day, as this statue at Alesia attests. In 52 B.C., Vercingetorix emerged to challenge Caesar and the Roman right to Gaul. Vercingetorix was able to unite Gaul's tribal factions against the Roman army.

In that same year, Caesar's daughter Julia died in childbirth. Pompey mourned the loss deeply, but Julia's death removed one of the key elements that had held Caesar and Pompey together. As his political situation began to worsen, Caesar faced a new foe within an old campaign ground: Gaul.

During the early winter of 53–52 B.C., Caesar appeared to have won virtually all of Gaul. Through the combination of his military ability, the valor of his troops, and his adroit diplomacy, Caesar had split the Gauls into numerous factions, each of which was too weak to oppose him or Roman rule. Caesar noted in his *Commentaries* that the Gauls were generally in favor of factional division which they believed prevented tyranny:

> In Gaul, not only every tribe, canton, and subdivision of a canton, but almost every family, is divided into rival factions. At the head of these factions are men who are regarded by their followers as having particularly great prestige, and these have the final say on all questions that come up for judgment and in all discussions of policy. The object of this ancient custom seems to have been to ensure that all the common people should have protection against the strong; for each leader sees that no one gets the better of his supporters by force or by cunning—or, if he fails to do so, is utterly discredited.

More than any previous Roman leader, Caesar had perceived this weakness among the Gauls and exploited it to his own benefit. But in the late winter and early spring of 52 B.C., a young Arvernian leader emerged to challenge Caesar and the Roman right to Gaul. His name was Vercingetorix, and he remains a powerful symbol to freedom fighters throughout the world today.

Vercingetorix must have been a powerful speaker because the Gauls respected the gift of oration at least as much as did the Romans. Gaul was full of tribal leaders, each of whom maintained some animosities toward some different tribal group. Vercingetorix soothed the hurts of many, and persuaded a large majority of the tribes to enter into a confederacy with him. The goal was simple: to throw the Romans out of Gaul.

The first action in the war—which Caesar called a "rebellion"—was taken by the Carnute tribe, located in what is now northwest France. The Carnutes were warriors, like all other Gauls, but they also made up a large percentage of the Druids who served as the priests and dispensers of justice throughout Gaul. Inspired by some of the Druids, the Carnutes threw themselves against a Roman garrison at Cenabum, on the Loire River. Cenabum was captured, the Romans there were killed, and the great Gallic War or Revolt had begun.

The Gauls had a method of communication that, while simple, was extremely effective. Rather than send courtiers on horseback, as the Romans did, the Gauls "shouted over the trees." The expression means that news was shouted from house to house, from tree to tree, and throughout the wooded areas that were so prominent a part of the landscape. It is believed that Vercingetorix, in the land of the Arverni, learned of the capture of Cenabum the evening of that same day, even though 150 miles stretched in between. The signal had been given; the war began.

Caesar hastened north from Cisalpine Gaul. By the time he reunited with his legions, Caesar found that at least half of Gaul was lost to Gallic control. Vercingetorix had done his work well; the Gauls stayed in their confederacy instead of splitting into the tribal factions that Caesar had previously manipulated.

The Romans consistently won the few skirmishes that followed. Following the advice of his Druidic counselors, Vercingetorix decided that hunger would force Caesar from Gaul. Rather than fight to defend some towns instead of others, Vercingetorix and the Gauls began to burn every village and town that the Romans came near. Within weeks, Caesar's men were hungry.

Vercingetorix's plan failed when it came to the town of Avaricum. The people pled for the right to defend their town, which was dear to them. Against his better judgment, Vercingetorix allowed them to fight the Romans. Not only did Caesar capture Avaricum, but the supplies he found there enabled him to face the coming campaign.

Now it was Caesar who held the initiative. He pursued

On the advice of Druidic counselors (such as the one shown above, at right), Vercingetorix adopted a policy of burning every Gallic village and crop in an attempt to starve Caesar's legions.

Vercingetorix so fast that the Gauls barely made it to the city of Gergovia in time to shut the gates. Gergovia was a mountainside fortress, and one of the strongholds of the Arverni tribe. Vercingetorix refused to come outside the city and try the matter in open battle. He kept his men confined to their fortifications, and he methodically planned his defense.

Gergovia was one of the few cities that Julius Caesar besieged but did not capture. In a rare display of insubordination, Roman legionnaires attacked the hillside on which Gergovia was based and did not heed the trumpet calls to retreat. The Gauls had placed stones and boulders there which they now pushed downward, crushing many Romans to death. By the time they pulled back, the Romans had lost about 750 men and many centurions.

Soon after the setback at Gergovia, Caesar began to march back to the province. He had seven legions with him, and his men were at a peak state of readiness. Vercingetorix misinterpreted Caesar's movement, believing that it was a true retreat. Under Vercingetorix's lead, the Gauls blocked Caesar's path. A major battle loomed.

Vercingetorix began the day's action by placing his 15,000 horsemen in front of Caesar's army. The Gauls had about a three-to-one ratio against Caesar in cavalry, and Vercingetorix believed this would be his trump card. Instead, it led to his downfall.

Almost as soon as the Gallic cavalry began its attack, Caesar made a counterattack. He sent about 1000 Germanic horsemen, whom he had recently recruited, against the Gauls. Faced by their oldest and fiercest foes, the Gauls panicked. Within an hour of its commencement, the battle had become a rout in favor of the Romans and Germans.

Knowing that his cause had become desperate, Vercingetorix led his Gallic warriors to a hilltop stronghold named Alesia (today the small town of Alise). Even Caesar was daunted when he first saw the white walls and towers of Alesia. He soon found answers to the situation.

Within two weeks of his arrival at Alesia, Caesar had his men build a wall that completely encircled the city. Vercingetorix could scarcely believe the skill and willingness of the Romans since they used the shovel and pickax as well as they did swords. The Gauls made numerous attempts to break the walls, to no avail.

Vercingetorix had the remnants of his cavalry make a nighttime breakout. Many cavalrymen escaped the walls and made their way throughout Gaul, summoning each and every Gaul to come to the relief of Alesia.

Knowing that Alesia had supplies for only one month, the

Gauls assembled an immense relief army; Caesar later estimated that it was 200,000 strong. Just as the defenders of Alesia were about to give up in despair, they heard the sound of trumpets (Roman) and the songs of the Gauls. The final battle for Gaul was about to begin.

But when the army of relief descended on the valley around Alesia, the Gauls found, to their astonishment, that the Romans had built an entire second set of walls. The second set faced outward, towards the relief army. Realizing what Vercingetorix's cavalrymen would do, Caesar had set his 50,000 men in motion, and in one month they had dug and built an entire second set of walls. It was one of the supreme examples of Roman military engineering.

The relief army attacked from the outside. The Gauls within Alesia attacked the inner set of walls. The attacks went on and on. For two days the relief army battered its head against the outer set of walls. Then Caesar took the offensive.

Once again, his German allies spread terror amidst the Gauls. Thousands of Gallic archers were killed by the German cavalrymen. When the last set of attacks against the outer walls failed, the remains of the relief army dispersed. No one could have fought harder or with more willingness than the Gauls. Caesar's leadership and Roman discipline were too much for them. The Gallic War was over.

Late in October of 52 B.C., Vercingetorix came out to surrender. He rode on a magnificent horse right up to Caesar and made his last public speech. Soon Vercingetorix was in chains, and Caesar had taken Alesia. He had won it all. The Gallic Revolt, as Caesar called it, ended quickly after Vercingetorix's surrender.

Caesar spared the people of Alesia because Vercingetorix had come and surrendered. The Gallic chief was taken to Rome and held as a prisoner for the next three years before he was executed on the day of Caesar's triumphal procession through Rome.

Although he put up a mighty battle, Vercingetorix had to surrender to Caesar in the end.

News of Caesar's victories reached Rome. Though the people of Rome had not seen Caesar in over eight years, they cheered themselves hoarse. Caesar was, without a doubt, the most celebrated leader of his time. Only those who recalled Pompey's successes in the previous decade could remember anything like the adulation that was accorded to Julius Caesar.

The question was whether even the city of Rome would be big enough for the two generals.

7

THE
CIVIL WAR

The beginning of the year 49 B.C. found Caesar at Ravenna, on the northeast coast of Italy. Caesar appeared happy and confident, but his closest advisers knew that horsemen were galloping from Ravenna to Rome and then back again, because Caesar was engaged in negotiations with the Roman Senate.

Ravenna is just north of the Rubicon River. The Rubicon served as the dividing point between the province of Cisalpine Gaul, of which Caesar was the governor, and the heartland of Italy. Therefore, even though he was a general and a statesman of great renown, Caesar could not legally cross the Rubicon going south with any of his soldiers. If he did, he would have to do so as a private citizen rather than as a general or consul.

This limitation was one of the important rules of the Roman Republic. Rome was frequently at war—sometimes with the Gauls to the north, and sometimes with the Spanish tribesmen to the

During Caesar's lifetime, Roman battle tactics evolved greatly. When facing an enemy city, Roman legions frequently laid siege, cutting off supplies to the city and weakening both her people and morale, before making an assault.

west. Roman generals accumulated great power during the course of their campaigns outside of Italy. To avoid takeovers and civil wars, the Roman Senate had long since decreed that it was illegal to bring any soldiers from the armies onto the Italian mainland.

Caesar needed to reach Rome, however. His political enemies had gathered against him in recent weeks, and they threatened to undo much of his work of the last decade. Envious of Caesar's battlefield successes, some of his enemies proposed that Caesar be brought to trial on charges of corruption and disobedience to the Roman Senate. It was imperative for Caesar to go to Rome and refute the charges. These many victories had brought Caesar wealth and fame, but they had also earned him many enemies. While Pompey was not an obvious enemy, he listened with great attention to those in Rome who spoke against Caesar, and it seemed now as if Pompey had joined the ranks of those who insisted Caesar disband his forces and return to Rome a private citizen.

All these matters came to a head in the first ten days of the year 49 B.C. Caesar left no diary or record from this time period. We can only make approximations of how and when he made up his mind concerning this perilous situation.

By January 7, Caesar learned that Rome was in a state of tumult. Pompey and his friends were running the day-to-day matters of the city while the Roman Senate was in a state of suspended animation. The tribunes, men who were elected to safeguard the interests of Rome's lower classes, had fled the city. It appeared as if Rome, which was so proficient at mastering other peoples, might fall to the divisions within itself.

It is likely that Caesar made his decision early on the morning of January 10, but he gave no public sign. Caesar was scheduled to attend a banquet in Ravenna that night, and to do otherwise would provoke suspicion because there were many spies from the different Roman factions in the town. Therefore Caesar went to the banquet, and, as was his way, appeared charming and hospitable to all. Years of social life as a young aristocrat and as Pontifex Maximus to the Roman people had given Caesar a sociable personality, and he played this card well on the evening of January 10.

Then, late in the evening, Caesar pled illness and left the banquet earlier than was normal. None of the spies around him took much notice; they may well have been drunk by this time. But, as was his trademark throughout his campaigns in the north, Caesar would act with stunning speed.

Caesar and a few companions left the banquet and headed on the road to their quarters. Before they had gone even one mile, Caesar changed direction, and the small group hastened to the banks of the Rubicon River. There they met nearly 1,500 of Caesar's most loyal troops, men who had been with him through years of campaigning. The rendezvous had been arranged prior to the banquet; Caesar had sent the secret orders sometime in the afternoon of that fateful day.

Caesar and his men crossed the Rubicon in the middle of the night. Morning found them well past the other side of the river; they had reached and occupied the city of Rimini. There Caesar paused. He had accomplished his goal of crossing the Rubicon. It was a decision from which there was no turning back.

Fifteen hundred men was a tiny force with which to invade Italy. Pompey had two legions totaling approximately 12,000 men on the peninsula, and he boasted he could summon thousands simply by "stamping my foot." Almost from the day that Caesar crossed the Rubicon, Pompey did not act like "Pompey the Great," the man who had defeated the pirates and Mithridates. As soon as he learned Caesar had invaded Italy, Pompey began to make plans to flee Rome. The conservative Senators, who had backed him just weeks before, now found Pompey was made of straw. On January 18, he abandoned Rome and crossed the peninsula, headed for the coastal city of Brindisium.

Since their commander had fled, Pompey's legions put up only half-hearted resistance to Caesar. His 1,500 men swelled

To avoid military takeovers, the Roman Senate had forbidden any general (including Caesar) to lead troops from a province onto the Italian mainland. By crossing the Rubicon River (the boundary between Cisalpine Gaul and Rome), Caesar sparked a civil war.

to double and then triple that number as he advanced south. Rather than march on Rome, Caesar pursued Pompey all the way to Brindisium. As he moved south, Caesar gathered the support of many townspeople and villagers along his way.

There was a brutality and a callousness about some of the Senators with Pompey that turned people against his cause and in favor of that of Caesar. But Caesar did suffer one notable defection from his ranks: Titus Labienus. Labienus had been Caesar's chief legate (virtually the number two man in command) throughout the campaigns in Britain and Gaul. Labienus and Caesar had collaborated on military plans and had been an excellent team. Now, as Caesar moved further south, he learned that Labienus had deserted his camp and joined that of Pompey.

Caesar arrived in time to blockade the city of Brindisium, and started to build siege engines. Rather than stay and fight, Pompey embarked what soldiers he had, what conservative Senators had chosen to remain with him, and sailed from Brindisium. Pompey crossed the Adriatic and landed on the northwest coast of Greece.

Lacking ships, Caesar could not pursue Pompey, but the entire Italian peninsula was now his. Caesar went to Rome and spoke before the Senate, the very body that had been ready to declare him an outlaw and an enemy of the state just six weeks earlier. Caesar made a magnanimous gesture, offering to make peace with Pompey if he would agree to disband his forces in Greece. Caesar asked a group of Senators to carry the offer to Pompey. When the Senators refused, Caesar quit Rome. Disgusted by the political process, he determined to seek out and destroy his enemy's support in Spain.

Pompey had been the proconsul for Spain for five years. One of his sons was in Spain, and several of his legions there declared for Pompey in the Civil War. Knowing that he could not cross the Adriatic Sea until ships were built, Caesar went by land to what is now Southern France and began the war against Pompey's forces in what was called "Nearer Spain" and "Farther Spain."

Caesar arrived at the city of Massalia (today it is Marseilles, France), where the Rhone River met the Mediterranean Sea.

Though they were not Roman citizens and had no special reason to favor Pompey, the people of Massalia resisted Caesar more fiercely than any Italian city had done. After two weeks of building siege towers and constructing battering rams, Caesar left the siege of Massalia to his lieutenants and hastened on to Farther Spain where Pompey's legions resided.

Though they were able troops and commanded by committed officers, Pompey's forces in Spain were not able to contain Caesar. He knew the ground well, having held a governorship there over 12 years earlier. As usual, Caesar made alliances with local tribesmen that allowed him to surprise and outmaneuver his foes. Within three months, the Pompeian forces had surrendered, and Caesar returned by land to Massalia.

The citizens of this city, who were of Greek descent, still resisted more stoutly than almost any fortified place that Caesar had ever encountered. After about four months of siege, the Massalians capitulated to Caesar. He might have wished to teach them a harsh lesson for their resistance, but he knew that it was more important to appear merciful than vengeful at the time. So he did not destroy the city, but rather accepted the surrender and hastened back to Rome.

Caesar found Rome obedient when he returned at the end of 49 B.C. His exploits in Spain had confirmed his reputation as a dangerous enemy. The Senate practically prostrated itself before him and voted him the title of Dictator for the duration of the Civil War. This was important because Caesar could now face Pompey with the support of the Roman government. Far from being an outlaw, Caesar could now claim he was the hope and savior of the Republic.

Early in January, Caesar made another bold move; perhaps it was one of the few times that he acted too hastily. Arriving at Brindisium, Caesar found that ships had been built, but only enough to carry about 25,000 men across the Adriatic Sea. Rather than wait for more to be built and for the better weather that would come with spring, Caesar made a daring crossing of the Adriatic Sea in winter. He arrived safely in northern Greece and immediately sent his ships back to Brindisium to ferry across the second half of his army. By then Pompey's fleet had been fully aroused. Pompey's ships blocked any further movement by sea, and Caesar's army was cut in two: half in northern Greece and half in southern Italy.

Caesar was in a difficult position, but Pompey made no move to attack him. The news of Caesar's many victories made Pompey extremely hesitant, and he failed to take advantage of the situation. Instead it was Caesar who moved against Pompey, besieging the city of Dyrrachium.

Pompey had about twice as many men as Caesar. Many of Pompey's troops were drawn from the eastern provinces which remembered Pompey's astonishing successes in the decade of the 60s. But Pompey allowed himself to be besieged at Dyrrachium. Caesar's men showed all their customary resourcefulness in digging ditches and building redoubts, and soon Pompey was blocked in.

Early in July, Pompey attempted a breakout. Not only did Pompey have twice as many infantry as Caesar, but his advantage in cavalry was even greater. Taking advantage of this, Pompey broke out from Dyrrachium in a one-day battle. Caesar lost over 900 men, many of them from the centurion rank.

Pompey's circle of advisers immediately named him "Victorious General." He was, after all, the first person to have won a battle over Caesar in many years. But rather than continue to contest the ground on the northwest coast, Pompey withdrew inland, with Caesar following.

The two armies moved at a brisk pace, and at the beginning

of August they were on a level area of ground on the border between Greece and Thessaly. The area where the two armies converged was called Pharsalus, or sometimes Pharsalia. It seemed an excellent place for Pompey to fight since the level ground would favor his cavalry force. Pompey seems to have doubted the wisdom of meeting Caesar in open battle, even after the partial victory at Dyrrachium. The circle of Conservative Senators who had accompanied Pompey to Greece demanded, however, that he meet and crush Caesar now. Just as important, General Labienus appears to have assured Pompey that this was the right moment for the decisive battle. In his *Commentaries*, Caesar attributes these words to Labienus:

> Do not think, Pompey, that this is the army which conquered Gaul and Germany. I took part in all the battles and my view is not put forward without consideration or based on facts beyond my knowledge. A very small fraction of that army remains; a large proportion has died, many fell victim to disease in the autumn in Italy, many have gone home, and many were left behind on embarkation. . . . These forces you see have been reconstituted from the levies of recent years in Cisalpine Gaul.

With the benefit of hindsight, we can assert that Labienus spoke a half-truth. True, many of the veterans from the Gallic Wars were dead or had gone home, but their indomitable leader and the core of his army—the centurions—remained. If Pompey were to win now, he would have to overcome the aura of invincibility that had grown around Caesar.

One of Caesar's centurions named Crastinus began the day saying, "Follow me, you men who were in my company, and give your general the aid you have promised. This is the only battle left; once it is over, he will regain his position and we our freedom." Crastinus then looked at Caesar and said, "I shall do things today, general, that you will thank me for, whether I live

 While Caesar was at war in Gaul, the business of running Rome fell to Pompey, who had the backing of many Roman Senators. When Caesar crossed the Rubicon with 1,500 troops, however, that support dissolved, and Pompey chose to flee rather than face Caesar's small but fiercely loyal army.

or die." Crastinus then ran forward, followed by about 120 picked volunteers. Crastinus' loyal attitude was something that Pompey could only long for. This does not mean Pompey was inadequate to the task; rather it suggests that Caesar had an extraordinary ability to coax loyalty from his men.

The Battle of Pharsalus raged all day on August 9, 48 B.C. Pompey began the battle well, with a cavalry charge against Caesar's right flank. Caesar had prepared a special reserve force—which, even though it was on foot, met and defeated Pompey's cavalry. Pompey's entire army then fell back to a wall of fortifications, but the blood was up in Caesar's men. They stormed the forts and captured them in the second part of the battle that raged all afternoon.

As the situation worsened, Pompey's mood gave way to panic. He tore off his general's uniform, mounted a horse, and escaped out the rear entrance of the fortifications. Riding hard, Pompey reached Larissa that night. Accompanied by only about 30 horsemen, he reached the coast of the Aegean Sea a day or so later and took a ship, first for Miletus and then for Alexandria, Egypt.

The day after the battle, Caesar received the surrender of thousands upon thousands of Pompeian soldiers. Many had been killed in the battle, but those who remained came forward and professed allegiance to Caesar. Knowing the value of clemency, Caesar urged them not to be downcast. He assured them he still considered them faithful Romans, and said they would be repatriated home as soon as possible.

Caesar also made a speech to his victorious soldiers. Caesar knew that these men were weary of war and of travel. They had been with him from Gaul to Germany, from Britain to Rome, and now to Greece. Now Caesar promised them that the war would soon be over. He mentioned generous grants of land and money to each and every veteran in the near future. These men did not forget.

Caesar then set off in pursuit of Pompey. Among the hundreds of men Caesar had lost at Pharsalus was the centurion Crastinus, killed by a sword thrust in the mouth. Whether Crastinus had a family, and whether any such family received money and honor for his action, is not noted. But Crastinus stands out as one of the few men mentioned by name in Caesar's *Commentaries*. He stands for the thousands of Romans who fought and died for Julius Caesar.

EGYPT AND CLEOPATRA

Caesar pursued Pompey first to Miletus and then to Egypt. Early in October, Caesar arrived in the harbor of Alexandria, located at the northwest corner of the Nile Delta.

Rome was undeniably the superpower of the Mediterranean world, but it still had competition from Alexandria. Founded by Alexander the Great around 330 B.C., Alexandria had become one of the major centers for learning in the Mediterranean world; teachers, scholars, and translators flocked to the Museum and Library at Alexandria. Then too, there was the architectural marvel of the Pharos Lighthouse, one of the Seven Wonders of the Ancient World. Built around 280 B.C., the lighthouse shone a light powerful enough to be seen 27 miles out to sea.

Caesar had never been to Alexandria, but he knew a good deal about its politics from afar. During his time as consul, and then while he was proconsul in Gaul, Rome had often had occasion to

Upon his arrival in Alexandria, Caesar was presented with the head of Pompey by Alexandrians who believed this a showing of loyalty to Caesar and Rome. Casear is reported to have wept at the offering, remembering the great man Pompey had been and their once close alliance.

debate its policies toward Egypt. The country of the pharaohs and the pyramids was no longer ruled by a native dynasty. Now it was governed by the Ptolemies who were descendants of Ptolemy Soter, one of the Macedonian generals of Alexander the Great.

The early Ptolemies had been capable military men and excellent administrators, but over the centuries the line had declined. While Caesar was in Gaul, the Ptolemaic throne was held by Ptolemy XII, usually called Ptolemy Aleutes (which meant "flute player"). Ptolemy Aleutes seems to have been a thoroughly incompetent ruler who enraged the people of Alexandria with his policies. Twice he fled his nation and went to Rome; twice he won over the Roman Senate which helped to reseat him upon his throne. Therefore, Caesar could claim with some legitimacy that he was not only a stranger chasing the defeated Pompey, but that Caesar had a right to arbitrate in the matters of Egyptian government.

Ptolemy Aleutes died in 51 B.C., and was succeeded by the joint rule of his daughter Cleopatra and his son Ptolemy XIII. Cleopatra was about 22 when Caesar came to Egypt; Ptolemy XIII was about 10 or 11. The brother and sister had recently gone to war with one another. When Caesar arrived, Ptolemy and his advisers held Alexandria, while Cleopatra and her followers were at a fortress on the eastern side of Egypt.

Caesar landed on October 2, and almost at once was presented with a gift: the head of Pompey. The advisers of Ptolemy XIII had killed Pompey upon his arrival so that they could present the head to Caesar as a gift and as a token of their allegiance to him. It is said that Caesar wept at the sight. Pompey had been his son-in-law, and Caesar remembered the former greatness of the man. Though he had been a lackluster opponent in the Civil War, Pompey had once been the greatest man in the Roman world.

His quest was finished—Pompey was dead. Caesar could have returned to Rome at once, and many of his critics suggest that he should have done so. But Caesar appears to have been interested in Egyptian affairs; he tarried a while, and during that time he met Cleopatra.

Virtually all sources agree that Cleopatra made a dramatic entrance into Caesar's life. Since Alexandria was held by her brother's forces, she had herself wrapped into a merchant's carpet as if she were the wares. The queen of Egypt was brought before Caesar in a carpet, and when it was unrolled, there she was.

Both the coins that were struck and the reports written indicate that Cleopatra was not a beauty. She had a large

Cleopatra, queen of Egypt, had to use her ingenuity to gain an audience with Caesar. Hiding in a rolled carpet to sneak past Alexandrian guards, she surprised and soon charmed the Roman leader. In the days that followed, the two became lovers.

nose and features that could change from benign to fierce. She also had consummate charm, feminine wit, and intelligence; she had mastered at least seven languages. Whether it was her appearance, her youth, or her ability to speak in Egyptian, Greek, and Latin, Cleopatra charmed Caesar from the first meeting.

The two probably became lovers within a matter of days.

Caesar had always been an amorous man. Cleopatra may have been smitten by the Roman leader, but whether or not she loved this man 30 years her senior, she needed his help. Cleopatra wanted Caesar to arbitrate between her and her brother, and hopefully to award the crown of Egypt to her alone.

Caesar was not initially inclined to favor Cleopatra's desire. It made much more sense to keep Egypt a land divided between the rule of two relatively weak rulers. That had been Roman policy until now, and Caesar was at first ready to continue that policy. But the advisers of Ptolemy XII, especially Achillas, the head of the royal bodyguard, decided that Caesar would indeed favor Cleopatra. Therefore they began to incite the crowd of Alexandria against the Romans.

Caesar had brought only about 3,000 men with him. It was a tiny force with which to defend himself against the Alexandrians, much less the entire Egyptian army. This was one of the times when Caesar's impetuous spirit and daring worked against him. Within two weeks of arriving in Alexandria, Caesar was a prisoner within the northernmost part of the city, surrounded by the Egyptian forces.

The Alexandrian attacks affirmed Caesar in his favor for Cleopatra. She became his political client as well as his lover, and her astute knowledge of Egypt made her an important asset to Caesar in his defense of the Roman position. In his *Commentaries*, Caesar described the physical location:

> The Pharus is a tower of great height and of amazing archi-
> tectural construction, standing on the island from which it
> takes its name. This island lies off Alexandria and created its
> harbour . . . Moreover, on account of the narrow channel, it
> is impossible for a ship to gain entrance to the harbour
> against the wishes of those who hold Pharus. This was
> Caesar's immediate fear, and while the enemy was occupied
> with the fighting he landed soldiers, seized the lighthouse,
> and stationed a garrison there.

Caesar and his 3,000 men were boxed up in Alexandria by about 22,000 Egyptians, led by Achillas, head of Ptolemy XIII's bodyguards. Caesar deployed his men in such a way as to maintain their position. His small group of ships also attacked the Egyptian fleet, using flamethrowers to spread fire amongst the enemy ships. During one such attack, flames spread into the city, and the famed Library of Alexandria was consumed in fire. We have no way to know exactly how many scrolls and volumes perished that day, but the Library had been the most important seat of learning in the ancient world. The Torah, which had been translated from Aramaic to Greek by the Library scholars, and other numerous great works were destroyed. It was a serious loss to Alexandrians, and an even greater loss for future historians.

Caesar managed to get messages out of Alexandria. Within weeks, Roman troops were marching from Syria on their way to Egypt. When the Roman reinforcements entered Egypt, King Ptolemy and Achillas broke off their siege of Caesar and went to meet the new foe. In the Battle of the Nile that followed, the Egyptians were defeated. The young king escaped on a boat that sank, and Ptolemy XIII drowned in the Nile.

Cleopatra and Caesar were triumphant. She was elated, believing he would soon chose to marry her and align Egypt's destiny with that of Rome. Caesar had other ideas. Fond as he may have been of Cleopatra, Caesar wanted to finish off the Civil War for good. He had to leave Egypt soon.

Cleopatra used all her charm and persuaded Caesar to take a vacation with her: his first vacation in at least 12 years. The Roman general and Egyptian queen floated down the Nile on Cleopatra's elaborate barge; it was equipped with all the comforts of the time, including no less than five restaurants. As they floated south along the Nile, Caesar may well

In a rare respite from battle and politics, Caesar was persuaded by Cleopatra to vacation aboard her elaborate barge, which was equipped with all the amenities befitting a queen, including no fewer than five restaurants.

have relaxed for the first time in more than a decade. He was victorious, he was in love, and soon he would be the father of Cleopatra's child. He learned of her pregnancy before he left Egypt in the early summer of 47 B.C.

However, the wars were not yet over. Despite his triumph over Pompey and his victories in Egypt, Caesar still had enemies to fight. There were still Pompeian troops in Spain. Closer to hand, though, was the danger presented by Pharnaces, the King of Pontus in Asia Minor.

Pharnaces was a son of King Mithridates, who had finally been defeated by Pompey in 65 B.C. Pharnaces was a sworn enemy of Rome, but no one had troubled to fight him during the early part of the Civil War. Now with Pompey dead, Caesar marched out of Egypt and then past Jerusalem on his way to Asia Minor (what we now call Turkey). Pharnaces marched south to meet Caesar and the two armies collided at

Zela. The Battle of Zela lasted only four hours; Pharnaces was completely defeated, and suddenly there was no further threat to Rome's eastern frontier. Caesar commemorated the event in a now-legendary dispatch to Rome, saying "Veni, Vedi, Vici," meaning "I came, I saw, I conquered."

9

THE LONGEST YEAR

When Caesar returned to Rome in the autumn of 47 B.C., he found three pressing problems: revolt, the Civil War, and calendar difficulties. In typical Caesar fashion, he attacked all three problems at once.

Over the past 14 years, Caesar had proved adept at recruiting good men for the legions—the centurion Crastinus being a prime example. Most of them fought for him with both discipline and ardor, but the time had come for them to be released. Prior to the Battle of Pharsalus, Caesar had promised many of his oldest legionnaires that it would be their last battle. Now he returned to Rome and found many of his best troops in revolt. Their pay had gone unmet, the terms of their enlistment had expired, and they wanted to go home.

The men of the Eighth, Ninth, and Tenth Legions were united in their determination—they had had enough of soldiering. Caesar

After returning from Alexandria, Caesar and his legions had more battles to fight. Not until all of Caesar's political enemies had been defeated could he discharge the soldiers who had served him so loyally.

went to Naples, where the three legions were stationed. He mounted a podium and addressed them in something like these words:

"Men of the legions. I understand you wish to go home. Very well, I release you. You are disbanded from your legions."

Men gasped. Caesar continued, "Not only do I release you from service, but I will make good on the promises I made to you after the Battle of Pharsalus. I will settle you on bountiful lands in the future, *after* I make provision for those legions with whom I shall finish this war."

Now men started to shift about, uneasily. Who knew what Caesar might do, or when he might do it?

Then Caesar began to speak again. He said one word: "Citizens . . ."

Now the shifting and grumbling turned into fear, almost panic. Someone shouted, "No Caesar, we are still your soldiers! We belong to you!"

Minutes later, Caesar accepted the renewed loyalty of all three legions. He had frightened them with his iron will, his apparent fearlessness, and with the idea that other legionnaires would earn greater glory and larger rewards in the future.

Danger from outside enemies was now over. Caesar then learned that the Civil War was not yet over. In the days and weeks after their defeat at Pharsalus, many of Pompey's soldiers had regrouped and moved to the west coast of Greece. Employing the fleet that Pompey had used, his shattered legions had taken ship for North Africa. Now, in the area that once was known as Carthage, Pompey's former army had been rebuilt to the size of about nine legions. Scipio, Pompey's father-in-law, was the new commander, and Scipio had found an ally in King Juba of Numidia. The Numidians of North Africa had long been known to Rome—sometimes as allies and sometimes as fierce enemies. Caesar knew that if Scipio had Juba as an ally, Scipio would bring elephants and the fast-riding Numidian horsemen into any future contest.

None of this news seems to have daunted Caesar. He left Asia Minor and took ship for Rome. Sometime in the autumn of 47 B.C., Caesar returned to the city had had so seldom seen in the past 12 years. There he was welcomed as a conquering hero and the savior of Rome. Celebrations were held, and the

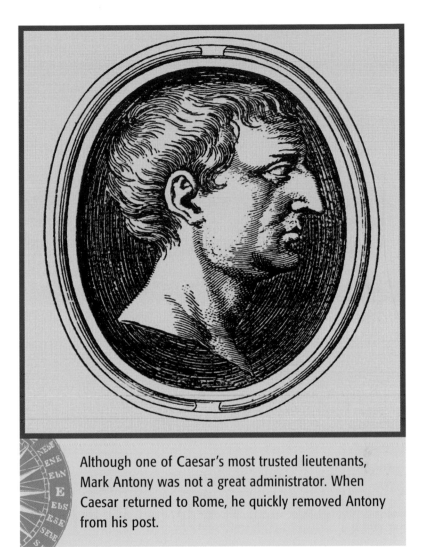

Although one of Caesar's most trusted lieutenants, Mark Antony was not a great administrator. When Caesar returned to Rome, he quickly removed Antony from his post.

Senate renewed Caesar's title as Dictator of Rome.

Caesar could almost certainly have remained in comfort in Rome. His legions and generals were by now so well-accustomed to battle that he might have sent them off to North Africa on their own. To do so, however, would have compromised Caesar's reputation, which was fast growing into a legend. He would have to go to Africa in person.

During his short time in Rome, Caesar found that Mark Antony, one of his most trusted lieutenants, was not a good

administrator. Antony had alienated many members of the
Senate, and a mutiny by some of the legions that guarded Rome
had occurred on his watch. Caesar therefore removed Antony
from his position and replaced him with Mark Lepidus, the
Master of Horse for Rome. Caesar sailed from Sicily toward
the end of December and was on the coast of North Africa on
the first of January 46 B.C.

Upon arriving in North Africa, Caesar found the situation
even more dangerous than he had been led to believe. Scipio
had compiled a very large army, and one of his most trusted
lieutenants was Titus Labienus. Caesar's former trusted second-
in-command had escaped from the Battle of Pharsalus and
made his way to Africa. Knowing Caesar's style of battle as well
as he did, Labienus was an excellent adviser to Scipio.

Early on in the campaign, Caesar and an advance guard of
about 1,000 men were trapped and cornered by cavalrymen
under Labienus. For several hours, the Pompeian forces rode
around Caesar's men, throwing javelins and taunting their
victims. Outnumbered and lacking fresh water, Caesar was in
what was probably the worst spot he had ever seen. However,
Labienus was wounded in the afternoon fighting, and without
him to urge them on, his men began to lose their spirit.
Labienus and his men rode off, having badly damaged Caesar's
pride and confidence, but the luckiest Roman—as men often
called him—was still alive.

On April 6, Caesar met his foes at the Battle of Thapsus.
Scipio and Juba had built a series of earthen fortifications on a
desert plain, and Caesar's men began the fight without orders,
forced into battle by events. Juba's Numidians made the first
major attack. Their movement was almost immediately shorn
of its largest aspect, however. Caesar's men confused Juba's
elephants by shouting, and then threw spears at the elephants'
flanks, hoping not to kill, but rather to enrage them. The
technique had been handed down from 202 B.C. when another
Roman general, Scipio Africanus, had defeated Hannibal's

Carthaginians at the Battle of Zama.

Not only did the elephants stop their forward movement; they turned around and caused great confusion in the Numidian lines. Caesar's men were trained to take advantage of such moments; they moved forward and inserted themselves into the openings caused in Scipio and Juba's lines. Soon the battle had become complete mayhem; because of the dust and noise it was often difficult to tell friend from foe.

Caesar's men excelled at this type of close, hand-to-hand fighting. By the time the sun went down, Scipio and Juba's forces were either destroyed or in full retreat across the desert. The battle was one of Caesar's greatest victories, though this time it had been won through the impetuosity of his men, rather than any tactical plan on his part.

King Juba committed suicide in the desert. Scipio escaped to the coast. When his ship was kept in the harbor by Caesar's ships, Scipio also took his own life. Labienus, however, escaped the battle, and disappeared for the moment.

Caesar was back in Rome by midsummer. The Roman crowds turned out in great numbers to celebrate his special triumph, commemorating his victories in Egypt, Asia Minor, and North Africa.

All was well—except for the Roman calendar. Caesar took the opportunity to introduce a calendar he had brought with him from Egypt. Based on the sun rather than the moon, this new calendar was accurate to within 11 minutes per year. In order to make up for the time missed during the Civil, War, Caesar prolonged the year 46 B.C. until it stretched to 445 days. In his book *Calendar*, David Ewing Duncan wrote, "The entire year of 46 B.C. ended up stretching an extraordinary 445 days. Caesar called it the '*ultimus annus confusionis*,' 'the last year of confusion.' Everyone else called it simply 'The Year of Confusion.'"

On January 1, 45 B.C., the new calendar took effect. Designed by the Egyptian Soignes, the new calendar had a year that was much more accurate than the previous one. Until then, Rome had to insert a thirteenth month of varying days every year in order to keep the calendar accurate. During the mayhem and confusion of the Civil War, no one had inserted the intercalary month, and by now the calendar and the seasons were off by two months. Caesar's new calendar, soon called the Julian, was one of his most long-lasting effects; it remained the primary calendar for the Western world until 1582, when Pope Gregory VII brought in the new Gregorian calendar that is still used today.

All seemed secure until Caesar learned that two of Pompey's sons had escaped the debacle in North Africa and set up operations in Spain. That, after all, had been Pompey's province for five years, and his sons, Gnaeus and Sextus, enjoyed considerable support. Making matters worse, two legions Caesar had left in Spain had deserted en masse, going over to the two brothers. Gnaeus and Sextus had already captured Cordoba and were winning over most of Andalusia, what is now central-southern Spain.

Once again, Caesar decided to handle the matter in person. He left Rome and marched through Cisalpine Gaul, the Province, and entered Farther Spain as autumn began.

Gnaeus and Sextus retreated before Caesar's advance. The brothers knew of Caesar's battlefield ability, but they too had aces up their sleeve. Soon after he arrived in Spain, Caesar was shocked to learn that two more legions had defected and gone over to the Pompeaian army. These were both legions recruited in Spain, and they were near the end of their tether. Caesar had made numerous promises of pensioning them off, and he had never lived up to the promises. Now some of his best veterans had joined Gnaeus and Pompey. Fortunately the Tenth Legion, Caesar's favorite, had remained trustworthy.

Even though he was outnumbered, Caesar employed his usual method: advance, attack, advance. The Pompeaian forces retreated before him. Several sharp skirmishes were fought

Generals and soldiers loyal to the slain Pompey joined forces with King Juba of Numidia (above) in an attempt to defeat Caesar. In the end, all of Caesar's political enemies were dead, either killed during battle or by their own hand after crushing military defeats.

before Gnaeus and Sextus decided to stand their ground in front of the town of Munda, in southern Spain.

By now Caesar knew that Titus Labienus was with the enemy, advising the two young sons of Pompey. Labienus had endured one failure after another since he had decided to fight against Caesar in the Civil War, but just one victory here in Spain might redeem all the missteps at Pharsalus, Thapsus, and elsewhere.

Whether or not Labienus was their chief adviser, the brothers chose their ground wisely. On the morning of March 17, Caesar's 30,000 men had to advance five miles across a level plain and cross a stream in order to reach the hillside where the Pompeians awaited. Caesar advanced with confidence, believing that the superior experience of his men would tell in any face-to-face encounter. The confidence was probably warranted; only a few thousand of the Pompeian forces were truly battle-hardened veterans.

The Battle of Munda began shortly before noon. Caesar's men advanced up the hillside to be greeted by waves of javelins hurled through the air. Many men fell in the first two advances, and Caesar observed his men wavering. There was no outright panic, but his men refused to advance again. Caesar is said to have seized a shield from one of his men and made a short advance up the hill. Inspired by their leader's bravery, his veterans sprang once more to the attack, and the Battle of Munda quickly became a hard-fought, hand-to-hand struggle.

Gnaeus Pompey ordered a large section of his cavalry, located on his right flank, to cross behind his infantry and reinforce the men holding the hillside. As soon as he saw this motion, Caesar ordered his own horses—7,000 in number—to attack Gnaeus' weakened right flank. Meanwhile, the Pompeian infantrymen were dismayed to see their cavalry make the move behind them. Believing that some type of retreat had been ordered, many of the younger members of the Pompeian army threw down their arms and fled.

Many stood and fought to the death. Titus Labienus met his end on the hillside at Munda. Thousands of Pompeians died that day, and the remainder were put to rout.

Now the Civil War was well and truly over. Gneaus Pompey was hunted down and killed a few weeks after Munda. His brother Sextus was pardoned. Caesar had no remaining military rivals. He returned to Rome to be greeted by the greatest celebrations ever seen in the city.

Cleopatra and her son Caesarion were now in Rome. Egyptians and exotic animals (such as a giraffe from Africa) competed with Gallic warriors and defeated Pompeains for attention. Caesar celebrated all his numerous triumphs in one immense celebration. It was by far the greatest ever seen in Rome.

The occasion was marred by two murders. On the day of his triumph, Caesar had the Gallic chieftain Vercingetorix executed. Such vindictiveness was not in keeping with the training of Caesar's youth. Second, Cleopatra had her younger sister murdered on the same day. Cleopatra wanted no one to come between her and Caesar.

10

THE REPUBLIC IS DEAD, LONG LIVE THE EMPIRE

C aesar returned to Rome at the beginning of 45 B.C. Many people found it difficult to believe that it was only four years since the Civil War had broken out. In those 48 months, Caesar had defeated Pompey's forces in Spain, Pompey in person in Greece, Ptolemy XII in Egypt, Pharnaces in Asia Minor, Scipio in North Africa, and Pompey's sons in Spain. This was, perhaps, the single greatest string of successes ever achieved by a Roman leader. When one added to this Caesar's prior subjection of Gaul and two invasions of Britain, there seemed little doubt that Caesar was among the greatest military leaders of all time. Only the record of Alexander the Great could rival that of Julius Caesar.

Clearly there was more to Caesar than military leadership. He had shown an adroit combination of mercy and forgiveness toward many of his foes; now, in the full flush of his power, Caesar wanted to change Rome itself.

More clearly than most of his contemporaries, Caesar recognized

With the end of Rome's Civil War, she was now well on her way to becoming a true empire. Although Caesar had unified the country and declared himself Dictator for Life, he publicly refused the crown of laurels offered to him by Mark Antony. The gesture set in motion events that would lead to Caesar's death.

that the Roman Republic was a spent force. Once it had been the best government available anywhere in the Mediterranean world, with its combination of consuls, senators, tribunes, and the like. That government had been designed to govern first a city-state and then to rule over the Italian peninsula. The Roman government had proved unable to manage the business of an empire, and Rome had truly become *the* empire of its day. The time had come for governmental changes to adjust to Rome's new position in the world.

First came changes in land ownership. Caesar was determined to provide for the legionnaires. He remembered the chaos that threatened Rome when Pompey's troops had not received their land grants in 62 B.C. Therefore Caesar proposed, and the Senate rapidly accepted, that new colonies would be created in North Africa and Spain, and that these colonies would consist of veterans who would receive regular payments from the state.

Then came the threat of political changes. So far Caesar had acted within the boundaries of his consulship and his temporary post as Dictator. But on February 14, 44 B.C., the Senate voted to make Caesar *Dictator Perpetuas*, meaning Dictator for Life. Caesar gratefully accepted the honor. He began to prepare for yet another military campaign, this time against the Parthians in Mesopotamia. They had crushed Marcus Crassus in 53 B.C., and Caesar wanted to punish them for their actions against Rome.

Just two days after he was voted Dictator for Life, Caesar presided at the feast of the Lupercalia. Caesar sat on a golden chair while the half-naked Luperci ran through the streets in their enactment of the fertility rites. During the festival, three of Caesar's associates, one of them being Mark Antony, came to Caesar and tried to crown him. Caesar took off the wreath and threw it among the crowd; this was the type of gesture that had always made Caesar popular. But there were some in the street that day for whom this laurel crown was a final insult. They now prepared to kill Caesar.

Though he was one of sixty men who conspired to kill Caesar, Marcus Brutus has been named and discussed the most of the conspirators. Born in 85 B.C., Brutus lost his father at an early age and had a substitute father in Staberius Eros, a Latin grammarian. Brutus went to Athens to complete his education, where he was influenced by the many Greek philosophies of the day: Academic, Peripatetic, Epicurean, and Stoic. Brutus was a serious student who took to heart the Stoic warning against undue emotion, either in joy or sorrow. By the time he returned to Rome, Brutus was considered a "coming man."

When the Civil War began in 49 B.C., Brutus fought for Pompey, because he believed Pompey was more likely to restore the Roman Republic to its former self. Brutus, like Caesar, knew that the old Republic was only a shadow of what it had once been; unlike Caesar, he hoped to restore and renew the Republic.

The day after Caesar won the dramatic Battle of Pharsalus, Brutus was brought before him. Caesar had a special interest in Brutus, considering him one of the most promising members of the younger generation. Caesar pardoned Brutus, and the grateful Brutus became one of Caesar's strongest adherents for the next three years.

Brutus never wrote memoirs, but had he done so, he might have indicated that he believed in Caesar the man, but not Caesar the King or Emperor. Once he decided that Caesar truly intended to complete the destruction of the Republic, Brutus became one of the ringleaders in the group of 60 men who would strike Caesar down.

Caesar rose early on the Ides of March (March 15). He intended to meet with a group of Senators in the late morning and then move to the preparations for his military campaign against Parthia. Caesar's wife, the faithful Calpurnia, begged him not to go to meet the Senators that day; she had had bad dreams and feared treachery. Caesar laughed off Calpurnia's fears, as he nearly always did. It was not that Caesar was blind to danger; rather, he seems to have known that he was a marked man and refused to cave in to the fear. Caesar had actually sent his best bodyguards back to Spain a month or so earlier; he did not believe that excessive precautions could save anyone from fate.

Caesar and Mark Antony went to the Senate House. Caesar walked in alone, reading a document, while Mark Antony was delayed by some of the conspirators. Once he was seated, Caesar was handed a petition for clemency for a relative of one of the Senators. Caesar curtly refused clemency, upon which a group of about 20 Senators came close and surrounded him. Caesar did not yet fear anything, but one of them put his hands on Caesar's shoulder and began to pull at his robe.

"This is violence!" protested Caesar.

In all, 60 men conspired to kill Julius Caesar. Their plans came to fruition on the Ides of March (March 15), 44 B.C., when 20 armed men, including Brutus, surrounded Caesar and stabbed him to death with daggers.

Then they came at him. Twenty men and twenty flashing daggers did their work. Caesar went down fighting, grabbing one of the knives and inflicting some wounds before he fell on the floor, his life bleeding away. As he looked up, Caesar saw Marcus Brutus with a knife in his hand. Caesar's last words were "*Et tu* (you too), Brute?"

Caesar died on the floor. The Senators, overwhelmed by their action, fled the chamber, and the body lay there for some time, undisturbed.

Caesar was dead. Who now would pilot the ship of state?

Cleopatra fled Rome. She and her son Caesarion reached Egypt and safety. Mark Antony delivered Caesar's funeral oration. A year later, Antony hunted down Brutus and Cassius, two of the men who had murdered Caesar. They took their own lives rather than surrender.

Gaius Julius Caesar was, beyond doubt, one of the most important figures in the history of Rome and of the Western world. In 56 years, Caesar created a new standard for military prowess; he was, and is, among the top military leaders of all time, on anyone's list.

Caesar also altered the political history of Rome. We do not know whether he ever actually wanted to become a King or Emperor, but we do know that he saw that the ancient Republic could not be restored. Caesar had lived through the Civil War of Sulla's day and had won his own Civil War. He had no wish to return Rome to anarchy.

Caesar's life and career represent a turning point: the point on which Rome ceased to be a Republic and became an Empire.

Caesar possessed to a supreme degree the following qualities: courage, capacity, vigor, speed, and ruthlessness. He had worthy opponents, many of whom had some of these qualities, but none of them encompassed them to the degree that Caesar did.

Caesar was, in many ways, the last ruler of the Roman Republic. His adopted son, Octavian, would become the first ruler of the Roman Empire. He and Antony were fierce rivals for Caesar's mantle. Finally, in 32 B.C., Octavian won the naval Battle of Actium and became the new Caesar. Antony and Cleopatra both committed suicide rather than become Octavian's prisoners.

Octavian, who later was called Augustus (the Revered One) was the unofficial ruler of Rome from 32 B.C. until his death in 14 A.D. Augustus never called himself King or Emperor (he preferred the title of "First Citizen"), but he wielded power as if he were. Upon Augustus' death, leadership went to his stepson Tiberius, who became the first Roman to take the actual title of Emperor. From 14 A.D. until the final collapse in 476 A.D., Rome was an Empire.

100 B.C. Julius Caesar is born in Rome.

85 Marcus Brutus is born in Rome.

84 Caesar marries Cornelia, daughter of Cinna.

82 Sulla arrives in Rome and becomes Dictator.

78 Sulla dies in Rome.

73 A slave rebellion begins in Italy, led by Spartacus and the gladiators who escaped from Capua.

71 Crassus defeats the slave rebels; 6,000 are crucified.

68 Caesar enters political life with his funeral oration for his aunt Julia, the widow of Marius.

67 Pompey receives a command to fight the pirates.

66 The pirates are vanquished.

65 Pompey becomes the first Roman to enter Jerusalem.

63 Caesar is elected Pontifex Maximus of Rome.

62 Caesar divorces Pompeia after a scandal involving her and Publius Clodius.

62 Caesar goes to Spain, his first command.

62 Pompey returns to Rome after an absence of five years.

60 Caesar forms the Triumvirate with Crassus and Pompey.

59 Caesar serves as consul.

58 Caesar becomes Governor of Cisalpine and Transalpine Gaul.

58 Caesar defeats the Helvetii and the Germans.

56 Caesar, Crassus, and Pompey renew their alliance.

55 Caesar crosses the Rhine and attacks the Germans; crosses the English Channel and invades Britain.

54 Caesar invades Britain for a second time.

54 Crassus dies while on campaign in Mesopotamia.

53 A Gallic confederacy is formed by Vercingetorix.

52 Caesar loses a battle at Gergovia, but defeats the Gauls at Alesia; Vercingetorix becomes his prisoner.

49 Caesar crosses the Rubicon River in northeast Italy.

48 Caesar crosses the Adriatic Sea. He loses a battle at Dyracchium, but defeats Pompey at Pharsalus; arrives in Egypt and becomes embroiled in the civil war between Ptolemy XIII and Cleopatra.

47 Caesar wins the Battle of Zela and writes to the Senate, "Veni, Vedi, Vici."

46 Caesar wins the Battle of Thapsus in North Africa.

46 The Roman year lasts 445 days.

45 Caesar inaugurates the new Roman calendar which is based on the sun rather than the moon.

45 Vercingetorix is executed.

45 Caesar defeats the Pompeian brothers at Munda in Spain.

44 The Senate makes Caesar "Dictator for Life"; senators attack and kill Caesar on March 15.

42 Brutus and Cassius are hunted down by Mark Antony in Spain.

41 Power in Rome is shared by the members of the Second Triumvirate: Octavian, Mark Antony, and Mark Lepidus.

31 Octavian defeats Mark Antony and Cleopatra at the Battle of Actium; Antony and Cleopatra both commit suicide.

27 Octavian offers to resign all his offices and retire, but the Senate begs him to remain.

14 A.D. Octavian dies; is succeeded by his stepson Tiberius, who is the first to call himself Emperor of Rome.

Balsdon, J.P.V.D. *Julius Caesar: A Political Biography.* New York: Atheneum Press, 1967.

Bradford, Ernle. *Julius Caesar: The Pursuit of Power.* London: Hamish Hamilton, 1984.

Caesar, Julius. *The Battle for Gaul.* Translated and edited by Anne and Peter Wiseman. Boston: David R. Godine, 1980.

Clarke, M.L. *The Noblest Roman: Marcus Brutus and His Reputation.* Ithaca: Cornell University Press, 1981.

Dando-Collins, Stephen. *Caesar's Legion: The Epic Saga of Julius Caesar's Elite Tenth Legion and the Armies of Rome.* New York: John Wiley & Sons, 2002.

Duncan, David Ewing. *Calendar: Humanity's Epic Struggle to Determine a True and Accurate Year.* New York: Avon Books, 1998.

Greenhalgh, Peter. *Pompey: The Roman Alexander.* London: Weidenfeld and Nicolson, 1980.

Holmes, T. Rice. *Ancient Britain and the Invasions of Julius Caesar.* Oxford: Clarendon Press, 1907.

Keaveney, Arthur. *Sulla: The Last Republican.* London: Croom Helm, 1982.

Leach, John. *Pompey the Great.* London: Croom Helm, 1978.

Meier, Christian. *Caesar: A Biography,* translated from the German by David McLintock. New York: Harper Collins, 1995.

Plutarch. *Roman Lives.* Translated by Robin Waterfield. Oxford: Oxford University Press,1999.

Polybius. *The Rise of the Roman Empire.* Translated by Ian Scott-Kilvert, selected by F.W. Walbank. London: Penguin Books, 1979.

Sihler, E.G., Ph.D. *Annals of Caesar: A Critical Biography with a Survey of the Sources.* New York: G.E. Stechert & Company, 1911.

Caesar, Julius. *The Battle for Gaul.* Anne and Peter Wiseman, translators and editors. Boston: David R. Godine, 1980.

Dando-Collins, Stephen. *Caesar's Legion: The Epic Saga of Julius Caesar's Elite Tenth Legion and the Armies of Rome.* New York: John Wiley & Sons, 2002.

Polybius. *The Rise of the Roman Empire.* Translated by Ian Scott-Kilvert, selected by F.W. Walbank. London: Penguin Books, 1979.

Bloggus Caesari—Julius Caesar's Weblog
http://www.sankey.ca/caesar/

Julius Caesar Web Directory of Online Resources
http://www.virgil.org/caesar/

Guide to the play *Julius Caesar* by William Shakespeare
http://juliuscaesar.future.easyspace.com/

page:

13:	Archivo Iconographico, S.A./ Corbis	59:	Bettmann/ Corbis
15:	Hierophant Collection	62:	Christel Gertenberg/ Corbis
18:	Bettmann/ Corbis	65:	Vanni Archive/ Corbis
21:	Stapleton Collection/ Corbis	67:	Bettmann/ Corbis
24:	Hierophant Collection	70:	Bettmann/ Corbis
29:	Hulton Archive/ Getty Images	75:	Archivo Iconographico, S.A./ Corbis
31:	Hulton Archive/Getty Images	79:	Bettmann/ Corbis
34:	Hulton Archive/Getty Images	81:	Bettmann/ Corbis
39:	Araldo de Luca/ Corbis	87:	Bettmann/ Corbis
42:	Gianni Dagli Orti/ Corbis	89:	Hierophant Collection
46:	Bettmann/ Corbis	93:	Roger Wood/ Corbis
49:	Hierophant Collection	97:	Bettmann/ Corbis
52:	Hierophant Collection	100:	Catherine Karnow/ Corbis
55:	Hierophant Collection		

Cover: Bettmann/ Corbis
Frontis: Hierophant Collection

SAMUEL WILLARD CROMPTON has a deep interest in the Classical world of Greece and Rome. He has written *Gods and Goddesses of Classical Mythology* as well as *100 Military Leaders Who Shaped World History* and *100 Battles that Shaped World History*. Mr. Crompton teaches both American History and Western Civilization at Holyoke Community College in Massachusetts. He has twice served as a Writing Fellow for Oxford University Press in its production of the 24-volume *American National Biography*. He has written several other books for Chelsea House, including *Waterloo, Hastings*, and *Tenochtitlan*.

ARTHUR M. SCHLESINGER, JR. is the leading American historian of our time. He won the Pulitzer Prize for his book *The Age of Jackson* (1945) and again for a chronicle of the Kennedy Administration, *A Thousand Days* (1965), which also won the National Book Award. Professor Schlesinger is the Albert Schweitzer Professor of the Humanities at the City University of New York and has been involved in several other Chelsea House projects, including the series REVOLUTIONARY WAR LEADERS, COLONIAL LEADERS, and YOUR GOVERNMENT.